The Featured

Ninja Cookbook UK 2023

1500 Days Ninja Foodi Multi-Cooker Recipes to Help You Discover
Even More Exciting Ways to Cook Your Favourite Meals

Billy Morley

Table of Contents

35   Chapter 3 Snacks and Starters Recipes

45   Chapter 4 Vegetables and Sides Recipes

55 Chapter 5 Soup and Stock Recipes

66 Chapter 6 Poultry Recipes

Introduction

The Ninja Foodi Max Multi-Cooker is a versatile appliance that can be used for a variety of cooking methods. It is a great addition to any kitchen. The cooker comes with a reversible rack, so you can steam vegetables or seafood. It also has a slow cooker function, so you can make soups or stews. The Ninja MAX Multi-Cooker is also very easy to clean, which is a huge bonus. It can be used as a pressure cooker, slow cooker, air fryer, steamer, and more. The Ninja Foodi Max Multi-Cooker comes with a 6.5-quart ceramic-coated pot and a 5-quart cook and crisp basket. It also includes a steaming rack, a Ninja Foodi recipe book, and a quick start guide. This book is packed with delicious recipes that are perfect for the Ninja Foodi Max Multi-Cooker. From breakfast to dinner, and everything in between, you'll find something to love in this cookbook. The Ninja Foodi Max Multi-Cooker is a versatile appliance that can do it all. It can be used as a slow cooker, a pressure cooker, or an air fryer. It also has a steamer function. The Ninja Foodi Max Multi-Cooker is a great appliance for those who want to have a versatile cooker in their kitchen. With this cookbook, you'll learn how to use your Ninja Foodi Max Multi-Cooker to its full potential. You will also get to know the fundamentals and maintenance of this amazing kitchen appliance. You'll be whipping up delicious meals in no time!

Fundamentals of Ninja Foodi MAX Multi-Cooker

Important Safeguards

The Ninja Max Multi-Cooker is the perfect appliance for those who love to cook. It is a multi-cooker that can be used to cook rice, pasta, chicken, beef, and vegetables. The Ninja Max Multi-Cooker is also perfect for those who want to make soup, stew, or chili. The Ninja Max Multi-Cooker is also great for making a pot of coffee or tea. The Ninja Max Multi-Cooker is easy to use and comes with a user manual. The Ninja Max Multi-Cooker is also dishwasher safe. When you're cooking, it's important to take some basic safety precautions to ensure that your food is cooked properly and doesn't pose a risk to your health. Here are some important safeguards to follow when using your Ninja Max Multi-Cooker:

· Read the instruction manual carefully before use.
· Do not use the cooker if it is damaged or malfunctioning.
· Keep the cooker clean, both inside and out.
· Do not use the Ninja Max Multi-Cooker if the power cord is damaged.
· Keep the Ninja Max Multi-Cooker away from children and pets.
· Do not place the Ninja Max Multi-Cooker on or near hot surfaces.
· Do not place the Ninja Max Multi-Cooker in a wet area.
· Do not use the Ninja Max Multi-Cooker if it is leaking.
· Do not use the Ninja Max Multi-Cooker if the pot is not properly seated on the base.

Parts and Accessories

The unit comes with a variety of accessories that can be used to help you create delicious meals. If you're looking for a versatile and convenient way to cook, the Ninja Max Multi-Cooker is a great option. This all-in-one appliance can be used as a slow cooker, pressure cooker, and steamer, making it a versatile addition to your kitchen. The Ninja Max Multi-Cooker also features a browning function, so you can brown meat or vegetables before cooking them. With so many functions, the Ninja Max Multi-Cooker is a versatile and convenient addition to your kitchen. The Ninja Max Multi-Cooker comes with a steaming basket that can be used to cook seafood, veggies, and more. The unit also comes with a frying basket that can be used to fry chicken, fish, and more. With these accessories, the Ninja Max Multi-Cooker can be used for a variety of cooking tasks. This makes it a versatile kitchen appliance that can be used for many different recipes.

Using Control Panel

Function Buttons

PRESSURE: Use to cook food quickly while maintaining tenderness.
STEAM: Use to gently cook delicate foods at a high temperature.
SLOW COOK: Cook your food at a lower temperature for longer periods of time.
YOGURT: Pasteurise and ferment milk for creamy homemade yogurt.
SEAR/SAUTÉ: To use the unit as a stovetop for browning meats, sautéing vegetables, simmering sauces and more.
AIR CRISP: Give foods crispiness and crunch with little to no oil.
BAKE/ROAST: Use the unit like an oven for tender meats, baked treats and more.
GRILL: Use high temperature to caramelise and brown your food.
DEHYDRATE: Dehydrate meats, fruits and vegetables for healthy snacks.
KEEP WARM: After pressure cooking, steaming, or slow cooking, the unit will automatically switch to Keep Warm mode and start counting up. Keep Warm will stay on for 12 hours, or you may press KEEP WARM to turn it off. Keep Warm mode is not intended

to warm food from a cold state but to keep it warm at a food-safe temperature.

Operation Buttons

The appliance has a number of buttons that can be used to select the desired cooking function. The following is a brief overview of the function buttons on the Ninja Max Multi-Cooker. The POWER button is used to turn the appliance on and off. The "TIME" button is used to set the cooking time. The "TEMP" button is used to set the cooking temperature. The "FUNCTION" button is used to select the desired cooking function. The START/STOP button is used to start and stop the cooking cycle.

Before First Use

If you've never used a Ninja Max Multi-Cooker before, there are a few things you should know before you get started. Here's what you need to know to get the most out of your new appliance. Read the manual. Yes, we know it's boring, but it's important. The manual will tell you everything you need to know about your new Ninja Max, from how to use all the features to troubleshooting tips. Clean it before you use it. Even if it's brand new, you should always clean your Ninja Max before you use it. Just run it through a cycle with some soapy water and it'll be good to go. Don't overfill it. The Ninja Max has a max fill line for a reason. Don't go over that line or you risk damaging your appliance. Be careful with the blades. The blades on the Ninja Max are super sharp, so be careful when handling them.

Install the Condensation Collector

One of the most popular items in the kitchen these days is the Ninja MAX Multi-Cooker. This handy little appliance can do it all, from cooking rice and steaming vegetables, to slow cooking meats and even baking cakes. And one of the best things about the Ninja MAX Multi-Cooker is that it comes with a built-in condensation collector.

What is a condensation collector?
A condensation collector is a small device that sits on top of the Ninja MAX Multi-Cooker and collects any condensation that forms during the cooking process. This condensation is then funneled back into the Ninja

MAX Multi-Cooker, where it can be used to help cook the food.

Why is a condensation collector important?
A condensation collector is important because it helps to keep the Ninja MAX Multi-Cooker clean and free of water spots. It also helps to prevent any water from getting into the food, which can ruin the taste.

How to install condensation collector?
If you've ever used a Ninja MAX Multi-Cooker, you know that it's a powerhouse when it comes to cooking. But one thing it's not so great at is collecting condensation. That's why we've put together this quick guide on how to install the Ninja MAX Multi-Cooker Condensation Collector. The Condensation Collector is a must-have accessory if you want to get the most out of your Ninja MAX Multi-Cooker. It's designed to collect any condensation that might otherwise drip down into the cooking pot, keeping your food nice and dry. Installing the Condensation Collector is a breeze. Simply remove the pot from the Ninja MAX Multi-Cooker and set it aside. Then, take the Condensation Collector and place it over the top of the opening where the pot goes.

Removing and Reinstalling the Anti-Clog Cap

If you love your Ninja Multi-Cooker but are tired of dealing with clogged vents, then you need the Anti-Clog Cap Ninja MAX Multi-Cooker! This nifty little accessory fits right onto your Ninja Multi-Cooker and prevents clogs by keeping food particles from getting into the vent. It's easy to use and clean, and it's a must-have for any Ninja Multi-Cooker owner. If your Ninja MAX Multi-Cooker is starting to experience clogging issues, don't worry - this is easily fixable! All you need to do is remove the anti-clog cap and give it a good cleaning. Here's how:
· Unplug your Ninja MAX Multi-Cooker from the wall outlet.
· Remove the pot and lid from the base.
· Locate the anti-clog cap on the underside of the lid.
· Use a Phillips head screwdriver to remove the two screws that secure the cap in place.
· Carefully remove the cap, being careful not to lose the small O-ring that sits on top of the cap.
· Rinse the cap and O-ring in warm, soapy water.
· Use a soft-bristled brush to clean any debris from the

small holes in the cap.

If your Ninja MAX Multi-Cooker is not functioning properly, one troubleshooting step you can take is to reinstall the Anti-Clog Cap. This cap is located on the underside of the lid and helps to prevent food particles from clogging the pressure cooker's valve. To reinstall the cap, simply unscrew the old one and screw on a new one in its place. Be sure to hand-tighten the new cap until it is snug. Here's how to do it:

· Unplug the Ninja MAX from the power outlet.
· Remove the pot from the Ninja MAX.
· Locate the Anti-Clog Cap on the underside of the Ninja MAX lid.
· Unscrew the Anti-Clog Cap from the lid.
· Screw on a new one in its place

Benefits of Using It

When it comes to mealtime, the Ninja MAX Multi-Cooker is a true powerhouse. This versatile appliance can do it all, from slow cooking and steaming to frying and baking. And with so many features and functions, it's no wonder the Ninja MAX Multi-Cooker is a favorite among home cooks. This unique appliance offers all the benefits of a slow cooker, pressure cooker, and steamer all in one. Here are some benefits of using the Ninja MAX Multi-Cooker. It is one-pot cooking, with the Ninja MAX Multi-Cooker, you can cook an entire meal in one pot. This means less time spent cooking and more time enjoying your meal. The Ninja MAX Multi-Cooker is a versatile appliance that can be used for a variety of cooking methods. Whether you want to slow cook, steam, fry, or bake, the Ninja MAX Multi-Cooker can do it all. It is perfect for large families. The Ninja MAX Multi-Cooker can cook enough food for up to 8 people at once. If you have a large family, the Ninja MAX Multi-Cooker is perfect. It's a time saver. With the Ninja MAX Multi-Cooker, you can cook an entire meal in one pot. This means less time spent cooking and cleaning up. The Ninja MAX Multi-Cooker can be used to cook a wide variety of foods. It's easy to use. The Ninja MAX Multi-Cooker is very user-friendly and comes with an easy-to-follow instruction manual.

Step-by-Step Using Ninja Foodi MAX Multi-Cooker

If you're looking for a versatile cooker that can do it all, the Ninja Foodi MAX Multi-Cooker is a perfect choice. This all-in-one appliance can pressure cook, air fry, steam, slow cook, sear/sauté, and bake – all in one pot. And with a 6.5-quart capacity, it's big enough to cook for the whole family. First, let's start with the basics. The Ninja Foodi MAX Multi-Cooker has a 6.5-quart capacity, making it perfect for cooking large meals. It also has a 1400-watt heating element, which means it can reach high temperatures quickly. The Ninja Foodi MAX also has an air fryer basket, a steam rack, and a reversible cooking plate. Before you get started, make sure to read the manual that comes with your Ninja Foodi MAX. This will help you understand how the appliance works and what safety precautions you need to take. Here's a step-by-step guide to using your Ninja Foodi MAX Multi-Cooker:

Select Your Desired Cooking Function/Mode: The options are pressure cooking, slow cooking, steaming, searing/sautéing, baking, broiling, and air frying. You can choose depending on what you're looking to cook.

Select Your Cooking Time: Depending on the cooking function you've chosen, you'll need to set the timer for the desired cook time.

Add Your Ingredients: To get started, simply add your ingredients to the pot. There's no need to pre-cook anything – the Ninja Foodi MAX will do all the work for you.

Stove Top: Assuming you have all the ingredients you need, the first thing you'll want to do is gather everything together and prep your ingredients. This means chopping any vegetables you'll be using and measuring out any dry goods like rice or quinoa. Once everything is ready to go, you can plug in your Ninja MAX Multi-Cooker and select the "stove top" function.

Heat Up: Next, you'll want to add oil to the pot and let it heat up. Then, you can add in your chopped vegetables and cook them until they're soft. After that, you can add in your dry goods and any liquid you'll be using (like broth or water). Once everything is in the pot, simply put on the lid and let the Ninja MAX Multi-Cooker do its thing!

Remove the Lid: Depending on what you're making,

the cooking time will vary. But once everything is cooked through, you can simply remove the lid and enjoy your delicious meal!

Swap to Top

In today's fast-paced world, we're always looking for ways to save time. That's why the Ninja Foodi MAX Multi-Cooker is such a great kitchen appliance. It not only cooks food quickly and easily but it can also be used to swap out ingredients. For example, let's say you're making a recipe that calls for diced tomatoes. But you only have whole tomatoes on hand. No problem! Just place the whole tomatoes in the Foodi MAX, and use the swap function to dice them. The same goes for any other ingredient you need to chop or dice. Not only does the Ninja Foodi MAX Multi-Cooker save you time in the kitchen, but it also makes meal prep a breeze. So if you're looking for a quick and easy way to get dinner on the table, this is the appliance for you.

Using the Crispy Lid

One of the best features of the Ninja MAX Multi-Cooker is the crispy lid. This allows you to cook food with a crispy, crunchy texture without using a lot of oil. Here are some tips on how to use the crispy lid:
· Preheat the lid by setting it to the "crisp" setting.
· Place your food on the cooking grate.
· Close the lid and cook for the recommended time.
· When the timer goes off, open the lid and check to see if your food is crispy. If it's not, close the lid and cook for a few minutes longer.
· Once your food is crispy, remove it from the grill and enjoy!

Using the Cooking Functions with the Crispy Lid

Air Crisp

The Ninja MAX Multi-Cooker is a versatile appliance that can do it all, and one of its best features is the Air Crisp with Crispy Lid. This feature allows you to cook food with a crispy, crunchy texture without using any oil. Air Crisp is perfect for those who are looking to eat healthier, as it eliminates the need for unhealthy frying oils. And, since the Ninja MAX Multi-Cooker can also be used as an air fryer, you can cook up all of

your favorite fried foods without any guilt. So, whether you're looking to make healthier versions of your favorite comfort foods or you're just trying to cut down on your oil consumption, the Air Crisp with Crispy Lid is a great option. Air Crisp with Crispy Lid in Ninja Multi-Cooker is a great way to cook food. The lid helps to keep the food moist and crispy. The lid also helps to brown the food. The lid is also dishwasher safe.
1. Preheat your Ninja Multi Cooker by selecting the Air Crisp function.
2. Place the food you wish to crisp on the air crisp tray.
3. Close the lid and cook according to your recipe.
4. Once done, open the lid and enjoy your crispy creation!

Grill

Grilling with a crispy lid is a great way to get that perfect sear on your food. But how do you do it? Here are some tips to help you get started.
Preheat your grill to high heat.
Place your food on the grill grates and close the lid.
Cook for the recommended time, flipping once.
Remove from grill and enjoy!

Bake/Roast

One of the best things about the Ninja Multi Cooker is its ability to bake with a crispy lid. This means that you can have perfectly cooked food with a crispy, golden brown top. Here are some tips on how to bake with a crispy lid:
· Preheat the Ninja Multi Cooker to the baking setting.
· Place the food that you want to bake in the cooking pot.
· Put the lid on the pot and make sure that it is locked in place.
· Set the timer for the desired cook time.
· When the timer goes off, open the lid and check the food. If it is not done, you can close the lid and cook for a few more minutes.
· Once the food is cooked, remove it from the pot and enjoy.

Dehydrate

Dehydrating with the lid on the Ninja Multi Cooker is a great way to preserve food. By removing the water content from foods, they can last for months or even years without spoiling. This process can be used for both fruits and vegetables and is a great way to have healthy snacks on hand that won't go bad. To dehydrate with the lid on the Ninja Multi Cooker, begin by washing and drying your fruits or vegetables. Cut them into thin slices, and then arrange them on the dehydrating racks that come with the cooker. Make sure that the slices are not touching, as this will prevent proper airflow and slow down the dehydrating process. Close the lid of the Ninja Multi Cooker, and select the "Dehydrate" function. Set the time for how long you want the dehydrating process to take, and then let the cooker do its job. Once the time is up, your fruits or vegetables will be dried and ready to store.

Get Started Pressure Cooking

Pressure cooking is a cooking method that uses high pressure and steam to cook food quickly. And with the Ninja Foodi Max, you can cook food up to 70% faster than traditional methods. Plus, the pressure cooking function has 11 settings so you can tailor it to your specific dish. One of the best things about pressure cooking is that it locks in flavor and nutrients. So, not only is your food cooked quickly but it's also packed full of flavor and goodness.

Installing and Removing the Pressure Lid

To use the pressure cooking function, the pressure lid must be installed. Here is a step-by-step guide on how to install the pressure lid:

· Make sure that the Ninja Max Multi Cooker is turned off and unplugged.
· Remove the lid by lifting it straight up.
· Take the pressure lid out of the box and remove any packaging materials.
· Place the pressure lid on top of the Ninja Max Multi Cooker, lining up the two tabs on the lid with the slots on the cooker.
· Press down on the lid until it clicks into place.

If you're like me, you love your Ninja MAX Multi Cooker. It's so versatile and convenient, and it's perfect for cooking large meals. But one thing that can be a pain is removing the pressure lid. Here's a quick and easy guide on how to do it:

· Start by making sure that the pressure release valve is in the "venting" position.
· Next, open the lid of the Ninja MAX Multi Cooker.
· You'll see two tabs on the underside of the pressure lid. Press down on these tabs and lift the lid off of the cooker.
· That's it! You've successfully removed the pressure lid.

Natural Pressure Release vs. Quick Pressure Release

There are a lot of different types of multi-cookers on the market these days. Some have more features than others, and some have specific functions that make them stand out from the crowd. So, which one is the best? The Ninja Max Multi-cooker is a great option for those who want a versatile and easy-to-use appliance. It has a 6-in-1 function that allows you to cook a variety of different foods, and it also has a quick-press release button that makes it easy to get your food out when it's done. If you're like most people, you probably don't think much about the pressure cooker sitting in your kitchen cupboard. But did you know that this humble kitchen appliance can be used for much more than just cooking food? A pressure cooker is a handy tool for natural pressure release. Simply put, the pressure cooker allows you to release pressure naturally, without having to rely on electricity or gas. This is perfect for those times when you're away from home and don't have access to these things. To use the pressure cooker for natural pressure release, simply place your food inside and seal the lid. Then, turn the pressure cooker on its side and wait for the pressure to release. This can take anywhere from a few minutes to an hour, depending on the amount of pressure that's been built up. Once the pressure has been released, you can then open the pressure cooker and remove your food. It's that easy! On the other hand, when you need to quickly release pressure from your Ninja Max Multi Cooker, use the quick-release valve. This will allow the steam to escape and the pressure to be released quickly. Be sure to use caution when doing this, as the steam can be hot.

Pressurizing

This process allows you to cook food faster and more evenly, giving you perfectly cooked meals every time. Here's a step-by-step guide to pressurizing your Ninja Foodi Max Multi-Cooker:

· Make sure that the cooker is turned off and that the pressure release valve is in the seal position.
· Add your food and liquid to the cooking pot, making sure not to fill it more than halfway.

- Close the lid and turn the knob to the pressure cooking position.
- Press the pressure release valve to the vent position.
- Set the timer according to the recipe you're using.
- Once the timer goes off, turn the knob to the release position and wait for the pressure to release.

Using the Cooking Functions with the Pressure Lid

Pressure Cook

Pressure cookers have been around for centuries and they are a great way to cook food quickly and easily. There are many different types of pressure cookers on the market, but one of the best is the Ninja Foodi Max Multi Cooker. This pressure cooker is a great choice for anyone who wants an easy-to-use and convenient way to cook their food. The Ninja Foodi Max Multi Cooker is a great choice for anyone who wants an easy-to-use and convenient way to cook their food. This pressure cooker is a great choice for anyone who wants an easy-to-use and convenient way to cook their food. The Ninja Foodi Max Multi Cooker is a great choice for anyone who wants an easy-to-use and convenient way to cook their food. A pressure cooker is a kitchen appliance that cooks food by using high-pressure steam. This high-pressure steam helps to cook food faster than traditional methods. Additionally, the pressure cooker seals in nutrients, making it a healthy cooking option. The Ninja Max Multi Cooker is a great option for those looking for a pressure cooker. It is a 6-in-1 cooker that can pressure cook, slow cook, steam, sauté, and more. It also has a built-in Ninja Foodi® TenderCrisp™ Technology, which allows you to quickly cook and crisp food.

Steam

When it comes to cooking, few things are as important as having the right tools. This is especially true when it comes to choosing a pressure cooker. If you're looking for a top-of-the-line pressure cooker, the Ninja Max Multi Cooker is a great option. One of the most appealing features of the Ninja Max Multi Cooker is the fact that it has a steam pressure lid. This is a great feature for several reasons. First, it ensures that your food will be cooked evenly. Second, it allows you to cook multiple items at once. Third, it cuts down on cooking time. Another great feature of the Ninja Max

Multi Cooker is the fact that it has a browning function. This is a great feature if you're looking to add a little bit of color to your food.

Slow Cook

You want to cook a tough cut of meat or stew until it is falling apart tender. The pressure lid also speeds up the cooking time, so it is perfect for those busy weeknights when you want a hearty meal but don't have all day to cook. Here are some tips for slow cooking with the pressure lid:
- Choose a tough cut of meat: Chuck roast, short ribs, or stew meat are all great choices.
- Season the meat generously with salt and pepper.
- Sear the meat in the Ninja Multi-Cooker before adding the liquid. This will help to create a rich, flavorful base for your stew.
- Add a small amount of liquid: Just enough to cover the bottom of the pot.
- Once the food is cooked, remove it from the pot and enjoy.

Yogurt

If you're looking for a delicious and healthy snack, yogurt is a great option. And if you want to make yogurt at home, the Ninja® Multi-Cooker can help. With the pressure lid, you can easily make yogurt in the Ninja® Multi-Cooker. Here's how:
- Add milk to the pot of the Ninja® Multi-Cooker.
- Place the pressure lid on the pot and select the "Yogurt" function.
- Set the time for 8 hours.
- After 8 hours, open the pressure lid and add your favorite yogurt starter.
- Close the pressure lid and select the "Yogurt" function again.
- Set the time for 2 hours.
- After 2 hours, open the pressure lid and transfer the yogurt to a container.
- Enjoy your homemade yogurt!

Sear/Saute

If you're looking for a Sear with a Pressure lid in a ninja multi-cooker, you've come to the right place. Here at Ninja®, we know that when it comes to cooking, every second counts. That's why we've designed our multi-cooker to not only be a powerful and versatile kitchen appliance but also to include a sear with a pressure lid. This unique feature allows you to sear meats and vegetables quickly and easily, without having to worry about the lid coming off and releasing all of the pressure. Plus, the sear with pressure lid also comes with a steamer basket, so you can cook multiple items at once. So whether you're looking to cook a delicious meal for your family or impress your guests at your next dinner party, the Sear with Pressure lid in ninja multi-cooker is a perfect choice.

Tips for Using Accessories

When it comes to small kitchen appliances, the Ninja Max Multi Cooker is one of the most versatile. With its ability to slow cook, steam, sauté, and more, this appliance can help you create a variety of healthy and delicious meals. To get the most out of your Ninja Max Multi Cooker, here are a few tips and tricks. Use the slow cook function to create hearty stews and soups. Simply add your ingredients to the pot, set the timer, and let the Ninja Max do its job. The cook & crisp basket is great for cooking vegetables, fish, and chicken. For best results, place your food in the basket and then add water to the pot until it reaches the "max fill" line. Sauteing is a quick and easy way to cook a tasty meal. To use the saute function, simply add oil to the pot and then press the "saute". Simply add your desired ingredients to the basket, then place it in the cooker pot. The silicone lid is perfect for sealing in moisture and flavors while cooking. It's also dishwasher-safe for easy cleanup. The removable cooking pot is durable and perfect for browning or sautéing ingredients before slow cooking. The recipe book that comes with the Ninja Max Multi Cooker is packed with delicious and easy-to-follow recipes. Be sure to check it out for ideas on what to make. The keep-warm function on the Ninja Max Multi Cooker will keep food warm.

Accessories for Purchase

There are a few different accessories that you can purchase for your Ninja Max Multi Cooker.

Cooking Pot

An extra pot so you can keep the Foodi® fun going when your other pot is already full of delicious food.

Multi-Purpose Silicone Sling

Easily lift ingredients and pans into and out of the cooking pot.

Multi-Purpose Tin

Create casseroles, dips, and sweet and savory pies, or bake a fluffy, moist cake with a golden top for dessert. D22cm H6cm.

Folding Crisping Rack

Cook an entire pack of bacon or turn tortillas into taco shells

Loaf Tin

Our specially designed pan is the perfectly sized baking accessory for bread mixes like banana and courgette. L21cm x W11cm x H9cm approx.

Glass Lid

See into the pot during multiple cooking functions, then use to transport or store easily.

Extra Pack of Silicone Rings

2-pack silicone ring set helps keep flavours separate—use one when cooking savory foods and the other when cooking sweet foods

Skewer Stand

Only compatible with the 7.5L models. Use the skewer stand to create kebabs. 15 skewers included.

Cleaning and Caring for Ninja Foodi MAX Multi-Cooker

First and foremost, unplug your cooker from the outlet. You don't want to be electrocuted while cleaning! Next, remove all removable parts from the cooker. This includes the cooking pot, lid, air fryer basket, and any other attachments. Wash all of the removable parts in warm, soapy water. Be sure to scrub any stubborn stains. Once the removable parts are clean, it's time to focus on the cooker itself. Use a damp cloth to wipe down the interior and exterior of the cooker. Finally, give the cooker a good once-over with a dry cloth. Make sure all water is removed, as this could lead to electrical issues. And that's it! You've now successfully cleaned your Ninja Foodi Max Multi Cooker. Below are some tips on how to care for it:

· Wash the removable cooking pot and lid in the dishwasher or by hand with warm soapy water. Do not use abrasive cleaners or scrubbers on the cooking pot as this can damage the nonstick coating.
· The Ninja Foodi Max Multi-Cooker has a stainless steel exterior. Wipe it down with a damp cloth as needed. Do not use abrasive cleaners or scrubbers on the stainless steel as this can damage the finish.
· The control panel is not waterproof, so be careful not to get it wet. If it does get wet, wipe it down with a dry cloth as soon as possible.
· The heating element is located in the base of the Ninja Foodi Max Multi-Cooker. Do not submerge the base in water as this can damage the heating element.

Cleaning: Dishwasher & Hand

If you have a dishwasher, you know the importance of keeping it clean. With all of the different parts and pieces that make up a dishwasher, it can be difficult to know where to start. Luckily, we've got you covered. Here are a few tips to help you keep your dishwasher clean and running smoothly. One of the most important parts of your dishwasher is the filter. Over time, the filter can become clogged with food and grease, which can impact the performance of your dishwasher. Be sure to clean your filter regularly to ensure your dishwasher is running at its best. In addition to the filter, the spray arm is another important part of your dishwasher. The spray arm is responsible for spraying water and detergent onto your dishes. If the spray arm becomes clogged, it can impact the performance of your dishwasher. Be sure to check the spray arm regularly and clean it as needed.

Removing and Reinstalling the Silicon Ring

If you own a Ninja Max Multi Cooker, you know that it's a versatile appliance that can help you create delicious meals. But one thing that can be a bit of a pain is removing the silicon ring when it's time to clean the pot. Luckily, there's an easy way to do it! To remove the silicon ring, simply twist it counterclockwise until it comes loose. Once it's loose, you can pull it off the pot and wash it in the sink. If you're having trouble getting a grip on the ring, you can use a butter knife or a small spatula to help pry it off. Once the ring is off, you can wash the pot as usual. Be sure to dry it

thoroughly before putting the silicon ring back on. When you're ready to use the pot again, simply twist the ring clockwise to secure it in place. Now you know how to easily remove and replace the silicon ring. If your Ninja Max Multi Cooker isn't working correctly, one troubleshooting step you can try is to reinstall the silicon ring. Here's a quick guide on how to do that:

· Unplug the cooker from the outlet.
· Remove the pot from the cooker.
· Carefully remove the silicon ring from the pot. You may need to use a small knife or other tools to help pry it off.
· Clean the pot and ring with warm, soapy water.
· Rinse the pot and ring well and dry completely.
· Place the silicon ring back on the pot, making sure it's seated correctly.
· Place the pot back in the cooker.
· Plug the cooker back in and try again.

Frequently Asked Questions

If you're like most people, you probably have a lot of questions about the Ninja Foodi Max Multi Cooker. Here are some of the most frequently asked questions about this amazing kitchen appliance:

What can the Ninja Foodi Max Multi Cooker do?

The Ninja Foodi Max Multi Cooker is a versatile kitchen appliance that can do it all. It can pressure cook, slow cook, air fry, steam, sear, and more. If you can think of it, the Ninja Foodi Max can probably do it.

How big is the Ninja Foodi Max Multi-Cooker?

The Ninja Foodi Max Multi Cooker is big enough to feed a family of four. It has a 6.5-quart capacity cooking pot and a 5-quart capacity air fryer basket.

How much does the Ninja Foodi Max Multi-Cooker cost?

The Ninja Foodi Max Multi Cooker is very reasonably priced.

Troubleshooting Guide

If you're having trouble with your Ninja Max Multi Cooker, here's a troubleshooting guide to help you get back on track. First, make sure that the cooker is properly plugged in and that the power switch is in the "on" position. If the cooker still doesn't seem to be working, try resetting it by unplugging it for a few seconds and then plugging it back in. If the cooker is still not working, the next step is to check the lid. Make sure that the lid is properly seated on the cooker and that the sealing ring is in place. If the lid is not sealing properly, the cooker will not come under pressure and will not work properly. If the lid is sealed and the cooker is still not working, the next step is to check the pressure release valve. Make sure that the valve is in the "sealing" position.

Helpful Tips

Are you the proud owner of a Ninja Foodi Max Multi-Cooker? If so, congratulations! You now have a powerful, versatile kitchen appliance that can help you create delicious, healthy meals for your family. Here are a few helpful tips to get the most out of your Ninja Foodi Max:

· Use the pre-heat function to get the perfect cooking temperature.
· When cooking meat, poultry, or fish, be sure to use the sear/sauté function to seal in juices and flavor.
· Use the slow cook function to create tender, flavorful dishes without having to watch them closely.
· The steam function is perfect for cooking vegetables and rice.
· The bake function can be used to create delicious, healthy desserts.
· The keep-warm function is perfect for keeping food warm until everyone is ready to eat.
· The delay start function is perfect for busy families

Replacement parts

If you need replacement parts for your Ninja Foodi Max Multi Cooker, you've come to the right place. Here at Ninja, we know that sometimes things break and that's why we offer a wide variety of replacement parts for our products. Whether you need a new lid, pot, or even just a new seal, we've got you covered. If you're unsure of which replacement part you need, our team of experts is always ready to help. Simply contact us and we'll be happy to assist you in finding the perfect replacement for your Ninja Foodi Max Multi Cooker.

Product Registration

It's important to register your Ninja Foodi Max Multi Cooker so you can receive the full warranty and other benefits that come with owning one of these amazing devices. Here's how to register your Ninja Foodi Max Multi-Cooker:

· Visit the Ninja website and create an account.
· Once you've created an account, log in and click on the "Register a Product" link.
· Enter the serial number of your Ninja Foodi Max Multi Cooker.
· Fill out the rest of the required information and click "Submit."
· That's it! You've now registered your Ninja Foodi Max Multi Cooker.

4-Week Meal Plan

Week 1

Day 1:
Breakfast: Cheese Polenta with Eggs
Lunch: Creamy Cheese Mushroom Risotto
Snack: Chili Pork Picadillo Lettuce Wraps
Dinner: Peanut Butter Chicken
Dessert: Oats Lemon Bars

Day 2:
Breakfast: Cinnamon-Apple & Butternut Squash Soup with Pecans
Lunch: Asian Quinoa and Carrot Salad
Snack: Cheddar Cream Bacon Beer Dip
Dinner: Balsamic Beef Roast with Potatoes & Carrots
Dessert: Cinnamon Fruit Compote

Day 3:
Breakfast: Strawberry Oatmeal
Lunch: Herbed Black-Eyed Peas and Greens
Snack: Orange, Apple and Pear Compote
Dinner: Apple Cider-Braised Kielbasa Sausage with Carrots & Potatoes
Dessert: Cinnamon Plums with Greek Yogurt

Day 4:
Breakfast: Garlicky Kale Breakfast Soufflé
Lunch: Brown Rice with Stir-Fried Vegetables
Snack: Cheese Artichoke Dip
Dinner: Creamy Herbed Chicken with Mushroom
Dessert: Vanilla Pear Butter

Day 5:
Breakfast: Cheese Pepperoni, Mushroom & Olive Quiche
Lunch: Simple Artichokes with Lemon-Garlic Butter
Snack: Classic Muddy Buddies
Dinner: Red Wine Braised Lamb with Tomatoes
Dessert: Vanilla Wine Poached Apricots

Day 6:
Breakfast: Coconut Muesli Stuffed Apples
Lunch: Barley & Beans Taco Salad with Zesty Lime Vinaigrette
Snack: Buffalo Cheese Chicken Dip
Dinner: Pork Chops with Creamy Mushroom Gravy
Dessert: Vanilla Almond Milk

Day 7:
Breakfast: Chocolate- Strawberry Breakfast Quinoa
Lunch: Spicy Lentil & Walnut Tacos
Snack: Spicy Black Bean Dip
Dinner: Lemony Chicken with Artichoke
Dessert: Blueberry Oats Crisp

Week 2

Day 1:
Breakfast: Homemade Blueberry Muffins
Lunch: Loaded Mashed Cheese Potatoes
Snack: Spiced Red Pepper Hummus
Dinner: Braised Short Ribs with Mushrooms
Dessert: Lemony Cinnamon Apples

Day 2:
Breakfast: Sweet Potato Hash with Eggs
Lunch: Flavourful Citrus Beetroots
Snack: Lime Hummus
Dinner: Spiced Pork Strips with Lettuce
Dessert: Easy Cinnamon Pineapple

Day 3:
Breakfast: Yogurt Egg Salad with Red Pepper
Lunch: Ginger-Garlic Bok Choy
Snack: Maple Barbecue Sauce
Dinner: Cheese Beef and Quinoa Bowls
Dessert: Classic Applesauce

Day 4:
Breakfast: Peach Oatmeal with Toasted Pecans
Lunch: Healthy Ratatouille
Snack: Savoury Tomato Ketchup
Dinner: Tea-Braised Eye of Round Roast with Leek
Dessert: Simple Strawberry Compote

Day 5:
Breakfast: Buckwheat Porridge with Mixed Berries
Lunch: Delicious Vegetable Shepherd'S Pie
Snack: Mini Balsamic Mozzarella Meatballs
Dinner: Spiced Pork and White Beans
Dessert: Tasty Peanut Butter Pudding

Day 6:
Breakfast: Cheese Spinach Frittata
Lunch: Lime Barbacoa Bella Burrito Bowls
Snack: Hot Sour Pepper Sauce
Dinner: Juicy Chicken & Broccoli
Dessert: Homemade Walnut Brownies

Day 7:
Breakfast: Parmesan Tomato and Asparagus Frittata
Lunch: Tasty Vegan Sloppy Joes
Snack: Lentil Celery Pâté
Dinner: Teriyaki Flank Steak with Mushroom & Carrots
Dessert: Red Velvet Cake Bites with Cream Cheese Frosting

Week 3

Day 1:
Breakfast: Sweet Apple Oatmeal
Lunch: Orange Wheat Berry Salad
Snack: Lemon Potato Puree
Dinner: Garlic Pork and Cabbage Stew
Dessert: Oats Lemon Bars

Day 2:
Breakfast: Banana Date Buckwheat Porridge
Lunch: Beans & Rice-Stuffed Peppers
Snack: Traditional Salsa Verde
Dinner: Barbecued Chicken with Simple Slaw
Dessert: Cinnamon Plums with Greek Yogurt

Day 3:
Breakfast: Cinnamon Banana Steel Cut Oats
Lunch: Creamy Turnip and Carrot Purée
Snack: Delicious Lemon Garlic Chicken Wings
Dinner: Country-Style Pork Ribs with Apple Sauce
Dessert: Cinnamon Fruit Compote

Day 4:
Breakfast: Savoury Spinach and Artichoke Egg Casserole
Lunch: Garlicky Kale and Potatoes
Snack: Cheddar Cream Bacon Beer Dip
Dinner: Easy Feta Beef Stew
Dessert: Vanilla Wine Poached Apricots

Day 5:
Breakfast: Delicious Coconut Almond Granola
Lunch: Quinoa Endive Boats with Pecans
Snack: Chili Pork Picadillo Lettuce Wraps
Dinner: Delicious Creamy Chicken & Brown Rice
Dessert: Vanilla Pear Butter

Day 6:
Breakfast: Strawberry Oatmeal
Lunch: Creamy Butternut Squash Mash
Snack: Orange, Apple and Pear Compote
Dinner: Ginger Beer Braised Pork Belly
Dessert: Vanilla Almond Milk

Day 7:
Breakfast: Cheese Polenta with Eggs
Lunch: Cider-Braised Lentils with Leeks & Apple
Snack: Cheese Artichoke Dip
Dinner: Lamb and Vegetables Casserole
Dessert: Blueberry Oats Crisp

Week 4

Day 1:
Breakfast: Garlicky Kale Breakfast Soufflé
Lunch: Easy Maple Glazed Carrots
Snack: Classic Muddy Buddies
Dinner: Spicy Turkey over Sweet Potato Boats
Dessert: Lemony Cinnamon Apples

Day 2:
Breakfast: Cheese Pepperoni, Mushroom & Olive Quiche
Lunch: Spicy and Juicy Red Cabbage
Snack: Buffalo Cheese Chicken Dip
Dinner: Smoked BBQ Beef Brisket
Dessert: Easy Cinnamon Pineapple

Day 3:
Breakfast: Coconut Muesli Stuffed Apples
Lunch: Herbed Aubergine, Courgette and Tomatoes
Snack: Spiced Red Pepper Hummus
Dinner: Ground Turkey & Black-Eyed Peas Stew
Dessert: Classic Applesauce

Day 4:
Breakfast: Chocolate- Strawberry Breakfast Quinoa
Lunch: Spicy Curried Chickpeas and Cucumbers Salad
Snack: Maple Barbecue Sauce
Dinner: Juicy Fiesta Chicken Tacos
Dessert: Simple Strawberry Compote

Day 5:
Breakfast: Homemade Blueberry Muffins
Lunch: Loaded Mashed Cheese Potatoes
Snack: Mini Balsamic Mozzarella Meatballs
Dinner: Savoury Beef Stew with Vegetables
Dessert: Tasty Peanut Butter Pudding

Day 6:
Breakfast: Sweet Potato Hash with Eggs
Lunch: Lime Barbacoa Bella Burrito Bowls
Snack: Lentil Celery Pâté
Dinner: Delicious Pork Chops with Apples
Dessert: Red Velvet Cake Bites with Cream Cheese Frosting

Day 7:
Breakfast: Yogurt Egg Salad with Red Pepper
Lunch: Flavourful Citrus Beetroots
Snack: Delicious Lemon Garlic Chicken Wings
Dinner: Chicken Feta Florentine with Spinach
Dessert: Homemade Walnut Brownies

Cheese Pepperoni, Mushroom & Olive Quiche

Prep Time: 15 minutes | Cook Time: 25 minutes | Serves: 6

Grass-fed butter, ghee or avocado oil, for casserole dish
85 g pepperoni, divided
5 large eggs
120 ml milk or heavy cream
1 tsp sea salt
1½ tsp (4.5 g) garlic granules
½ tsp onion powder
½ tsp dried oregano
½ tsp dried thyme
3 small tomatoes, seeded and chopped
15 g chopped fresh flat-leaf parsley
70 g sliced mushrooms
50 g pitted and sliced black olives
115 g shredded mozzarella cheese
40 g shredded Parmesan cheese
240 ml water

1. Grease a casserole dish that fits inside the pot with oil. Set it aside. 2. Chop 28g of the pepperoni, reserving the remaining pepperoni (left whole). 3. In a large bowl, whisk together the eggs and milk. Add the salt, onion powder, garlic granules, thyme, oregano, parsley, mushrooms, tomatoes, olives, the chopped pepperoni and the cheeses, gently stirring to combine. 4. Pour the mixture into the prepared casserole dish. In a uniform layer, place the remaining whole pieces of pepperoni on top of the filling. 5. Cover the casserole dish with its glass lid or you can cover the top of the dish with unbleached parchment paper, then put foil on top and secure it around the edges. 6. Pour water into the pot and place the bottom layer of the Deluxe Reversible Rack in the lower position in the pot. Carefully place the covered casserole dish on top of the rack. 7. Close the lid and move slider to PRESSURE. Make sure the pressure release valve is in the SEAL position. The temperature will default to HIGH, which is the correct setting. Set time to 25 minutes. Select START/STOP to begin cooking. 8. When cooking is complete, naturally release the pressure for 10 minutes. Then turn the pressure relief valve to the VENT position for quick pressure relief. Move slider to AIR FRY/ STOVETOP to unlock the lid, then carefully open it. 9. Carefully remove the casserole dish from the pot and remove the lid from the dish. 10. Lest it rest for 15 minutes, serve.

Per Serving: Calories 241; Fat 18.02g; Sodium 947mg; Carbs 5.15g; Fibre 1.2g; Sugar 1.93g; Protein 14.8g

Strawberry Oatmeal

Prep Time: 10 minutes | Cook Time: 3 minutes | Serves: 4

240 ml plain unsweetened almond milk
240 ml water
80 g old-fashioned rolled oats
¼ tsp salt
1 cinnamon stick

45 g cream cheese, softened
½ tsp pure vanilla extract
170 g sliced strawberries
25 g crumbled digestive biscuits
Honey, for drizzling

1. Add the almond milk, water, oats, cinnamon stick and salt to the pot and stir to mix well. 2. Close the lid and move slider to PRESSURE. Make sure the pressure release valve is in the SEAL position. The temperature will default to HIGH, which is the correct setting. Set time to 3 minutes. Select START/STOP to begin cooking. 3. When cooking is complete, naturally release the pressure for 20 minutes. Then turn the pressure relief valve to the VENT position for quick pressure relief. Move slider to AIR FRY/ STOVETOP to unlock the lid, then carefully open it. 4. Stir in the oats and remove the cinnamon stick. 5. Add the cream cheese and vanilla. Stir until the cream cheese is completely melted into the oats. 6. Place the cooked oats in four serving bowls and top with strawberries, digestive biscuits and a drizzle of honey.

Per Serving: Calories 508; Fat 39.6g; Sodium 341mg; Carbs 36.11g; Fibre 11.2g; Sugar 11.02g; Protein 18.27g

Chocolate– Strawberry Breakfast Quinoa

Prep Time: 5 minutes | Cook Time: 12 minutes | Serves: 2

80 g uncooked quinoa
180 ml unsweetened coconut milk, plus more for serving
120 ml water
2 tablespoons maple syrup

1 tablespoon unsweetened cocoa powder
½ teaspoon vanilla extract (optional)
Pinch salt
30 g fresh strawberries
25 g chocolate shavings

1. Rinse the quinoa in a fine-mesh strainer for 2 minutes. Sort and pick out any discoloured pieces or pebbles by your hands. 2. Put the quinoa in the bowl and stir in the water, coconut milk, cocoa powder, maple syrup, vanilla (if using), and salt. 3. Close the lid and move slider to PRESSURE. Make sure the pressure release valve is in the SEAL position. Set the temperature to LOW and set time to 12 minutes. Select START/STOP to begin cooking. 4. When cooking is complete, naturally release the pressure for 10 minutes. Then turn the pressure relief valve to the VENT position for quick pressure relief. Move slider to AIR FRY/ STOVETOP to unlock the lid, then carefully open it. 5. Fluff the quinoa with a fork and spoon it into two cereal bowls. Add more coconut milk, and top with strawberries and chocolate shavings.

Per Serving: Calories 535; Fat 24.88g; Sodium 280mg; Carbs 73.16g; Fibre 7.1g; Sugar 34.78g; Protein 9.47g

Garlicky Kale Breakfast Soufflé

Prep Time: 15 minutes | Cook Time: 10 minutes | Serves: 4

1 tbsp (15 ml) extra-virgin olive oil
½ yellow onion, diced
135 g trimmed and chopped kale
Salt
Freshly ground black pepper

1 clove garlic, grated
240 ml water
Unsalted butter, for ramekins
4 large eggs
2 tsp (10 ml) heavy cream

1. Move slider to AIR FRY/STOVETOP. Select SEAR/SAUTÉ and set to 3. Select START/STOP to begin preheating. Allow unit to preheat for 5 minutes. After 5 minutes, add the olive oil. Heat the oil for 1 minute, then add the onion. Sauté for 2 minutes. 2. Mix in the kale and season with a little salt and pepper. Sauté for 3 to 4 minutes, or until tender and slightly wilted. Add the garlic, stir to combine and sauté for one more minute. Press START/STOP to turn off the SEAR/SAUTÉ function. 3. Remove the kale mixture and transfer to a small plate. 4. Clean the pot and return it to the device. Pour the water into the pot and place the bottom layer of the Deluxe Reversible Rack in the lower position in the pot. 5. Butter four small soufflé ramekins with unsalted butter. Place a little bit of the kale mixture in the bottom of each ramekin. 6. Crack an egg into each ramekin, then top each egg with ½ teaspoon of the heavy cream and sprinkle with salt and pepper. Place the ramekins on the rack. 7. Close the lid and move slider to PRESSURE. Make sure the pressure release valve is in the SEAL position. The temperature will default to HIGH, which is the correct setting. Set time to 3 minutes. Select START/STOP to begin cooking. 8. When the timer beeps, naturally release the pressure for 2 minutes. Then turn the pressure relief valve to the VENT position for quick pressure relief. Move slider to AIR FRY/ STOVETOP to unlock the lid, then carefully open it.
Per Serving: Calories 112; Fat 8.97g; Sodium 163mg; Carbs 4.83g; Fibre 0.7g; Sugar 2.43g; Protein 3.52g

Cinnamon–Apple & Butternut Squash Soup with Pecans

Prep Time: 10 minutes | Cook Time: 6 minutes | Serves: 4

430 g seeded, peeled and cut butternut squash (1.3-cm chunks)
1 apple, peeled, cored and cut into 1.3-cm chunks (I like Honeycrisp or Gala apples)
1 (400-ml) can full-fat coconut milk

2 tsp (5 g) ground cinnamon
1 tbsp (15 ml) pure maple syrup
Pinch of salt
55 g roasted and chopped pecans

1. Add the butternut squash, apple pieces, cinnamon, coconut milk, maple syrup and salt to the pot and stir to mix well. 2. Close the lid and move slider to PRESSURE. Make sure the pressure release valve is in the SEAL position. The temperature will default to HIGH, which is the correct setting. Set time to 6 minutes. Select START/STOP to begin cooking. 3. When cooking is complete, turn the pressure relief valve to the VENT position for quick pressure relief. Move slider to the right to unlock the lid, then carefully open it. 4. Using an immersion blender or high-powered blender, blend until smooth. 5. Serve warm and top with pecans.
Per Serving: Calories 372; Fat 33.29g; Sodium 163mg; Carbs 20.85g; Fibre 6.1g; Sugar 13.52g; Protein 4.65g

Homemade Blueberry Muffins

Prep Time: 10 minutes | Cook Time: 10 minutes | Serves: 6

Nonstick cooking spray
125 g spelt flour
1 teaspoon baking powder
¼ teaspoon baking soda
⅛ teaspoon salt
1 egg, beaten

3 tablespoons nondairy milk
2 tablespoons coconut oil, melted
2 tablespoons honey
1 teaspoon vanilla extract
60 g fresh or frozen blueberries

1. Grease the outer 6 wells of a 7-well silicone egg bite mold with nonstick cooking spray. 2. In a medium bowl, mix together the flour, baking soda, baking powder, and salt. 3. In a small bowl, whisk the egg, coconut oil, milk, honey, and vanilla. Add the egg mixture to the flour mixture and stir until combined into a thick batter. 4. Divide the batter between the prepared egg bite wells, filling each well about halfway. Gently press the blueberries into the top of each muffin. Place the lid on the mold. 5. Pour 240 ml of water into the pot and place the bottom layer of the Deluxe Reversible Rack in the lower position in the pot. Place the egg bite mold on the rack. 6. Close the lid and move slider to PRESSURE. Make sure the pressure release valve is in the SEAL position. The temperature will default to HIGH, which is the correct setting. Set time to 10 minutes. Select START/STOP to begin cooking. 7. When the cook time is complete, let the pressure release naturally for 10 minutes, then quick release any remaining pressure. 8. Open the lid carefully and lift out the mold. Uncover the muffins and let them rest for 3 to 5 minutes, until the mold is cool to the touch, then pop the muffins out. 9. Serve warm or store at room temperature in an airtight container for up to 3 days.

Per Serving: Calories 194; Fat 7.22g; Sodium 130mg; Carbs 28.71g; Fibre 3.5g; Sugar 9.39g; Protein 6.03g

Coconut Muesli Stuffed Apples

Prep Time: 10 minutes | Cook Time: 3 minutes | Serves: 2

2 large unpeeled organic apples, cored
40 g coconut muesli
2 tablespoons butter, cubed

2 teaspoons packed brown sugar
½ teaspoon ground cinnamon
80 ml water

1. Remove the tops of the apples and slice the bottoms off just enough to help the apples sit flat in the cooker pot. 2. In a medium bowl, combine the muesli, brown sugar, butter, and cinnamon, mashing gently with a fork until combined. 3. Stuff each apple with the muesli mixture, then place them in the bottom of the cooker pot. Add the water to the pot. 4. Close the lid and move slider to PRESSURE. Make sure the pressure release valve is in the SEAL position. Set the heat to LOW and set time to 3 minutes. Select START/STOP to begin cooking. 5. When cooking is complete, naturally release the pressure for 10 minutes. Then turn the pressure relief valve to the VENT position for quick pressure relief. Move slider to AIR FRY/ STOVETOP to unlock the lid, then carefully open it. 6. Serve with Greek yogurt.

Per Serving: Calories 241; Fat 12.02g; Sodium 157mg; Carbs 36.05g; Fibre 6.4g; Sugar 27.2g; Protein 1.16g

Sweet Potato Hash with Eggs

Prep Time: 10 minutes | Cook Time: 13 minutes | Serves: 4

✦✦✦✦✦✦

1 tablespoon olive oil
675 g sweet potatoes, peeled and diced
1 yellow onion, chopped
1 red pepper , seeded and chopped
2 garlic cloves, minced
1 teaspoon dried oregano

½ teaspoon cayenne pepper
½ teaspoon salt
¼ teaspoon freshly ground black pepper
120 ml vegetable stock or store-bought low-sodium vegetable stock
4 large eggs

✦✦✦✦✦✦

1. Move slider to AIR FRY/STOVETOP. Select SEAR/SAUTÉ and set to 3. Select START/STOP to begin preheating. Allow unit to preheat for 5 minutes. After 5 minutes, add the olive oil. When the oil is hot, add the sweet potatoes and sauté for 10 minutes, stirring occasionally, until the potatoes begin to brown and soften. 2. Stir in the onion, pepper , garlic, cayenne pepper, oregano, salt, and black pepper until well combined. Press START/STOP to turn off the SEAR/SAUTÉ function. 3. Stir in the stock, then crack the eggs on top of the potato mixture. Close the lid. 4. Move slider to PRESSURE. Make sure the pressure release valve is in the SEAL position. The temperature will default to HIGH, which is the correct setting. Set time to 3 minutes. Select START/STOP to begin cooking. 5. When the cook time is complete, quick release the pressure. 6. Carefully open the lid and serve.

Per Serving: Calories 199; Fat 11.32g; Sodium 331mg; Carbs 20.42g; Fibre 9.9g; Sugar 2.59g; Protein 7.8g

Sweet Apple Oatmeal

Prep Time: 10 minutes | Cook Time: 8 minutes | Serves: 4

✦✦✦✦✦✦

1 tablespoon light olive oil
1 large Granny Smith, Honeycrisp, or Pink Lady apple, peeled, cored, and diced
½ teaspoon ground cardamom

80 g steel-cut oats
720 g water
55 g maple syrup
½ teaspoon salt

✦✦✦✦✦✦

1. Move slider to AIR FRY/STOVETOP. Select SEAR/SAUTÉ and set to 3. Select START/STOP to begin cooking. Heat oil in the pot, then add apple and cardamom and cook until apple is just softened, about 2 minutes. Press START/STOP to turn off the SEAR/SAUTÉ function. 2. Add water, oats, maple syrup, and salt to pot, and stir well. 3. Close the lid and move slider to PRESSURE. Make sure the pressure release valve is in the SEAL position. The temperature will default to HIGH, which is the correct setting. Set time to 5 minutes. Select START/STOP to begin cooking. 4. When cooking is complete, naturally release the pressure for 10 minutes. Then turn the pressure relief valve to the VENT position for quick pressure relief. Move slider to AIR FRY/ STOVETOP to unlock the lid, then carefully open it. Stir well. Serve hot.

Per Serving: Calories 170; Fat 5.15g; Sodium 298mg; Carbs 35.95g; Fibre 5.1g; Sugar 17.19g; Protein 4.33g

Yogurt Egg Salad with Red Pepper

Prep Time: 10 minutes | Cook Time: 10 minutes | Serves: 6

6 large eggs

240 ml water

1 tablespoon olive oil

1 medium red pepper , seeded and chopped

¼ teaspoon salt

¼ teaspoon ground black pepper

120 g low-fat plain Greek yogurt

2 tablespoons chopped fresh dill

1. Fill a large bowl with ice water. Place the bottom layer of the Deluxe Reversible Rack in the lower position in the pot. 2. Arrange eggs on rack and add water to the pot. Close the lid. 3. Close the lid and move slider to PRESSURE. Make sure the pressure release valve is in the SEAL position. The temperature will default to HIGH, which is the correct setting. Set time to 5 minutes. Select START/STOP to begin cooking. 4. When cooking is complete, naturally release the pressure for 5 minutes. Then turn the pressure relief valve to the VENT position for quick pressure relief. Move slider to AIR FRY/ STOVETOP to unlock the lid, then carefully open it. 5. Carefully transfer eggs to the bowl of ice water. Let stand in ice water for 10 minutes, then peel, chop, and add eggs to a medium bowl. 6. Clean out pot, dry well, and return to machine. Move slider to AIR FRY/STOVETOP. Select SEAR/SAUTÉ and set to 3. Select START/STOP to begin cooking. Heat oil in the pot. Add pepper , salt, and black pepper. Cook, stirring frequently, until pepper is tender, about 5 minutes. Transfer to bowl with eggs. 7. Add yogurt and dill to bowl, and fold to combine. Cover and chill for 1 hour before serving.

Per Serving: Calories 101; Fat 7.46g; Sodium 122mg; Carbs 4.64g; Fibre 0.9g; Sugar 2.46g; Protein 4.35g

Peach Oatmeal with Toasted Pecans

Prep Time: 10 minutes | Cook Time: 4 minutes | Serves: 4

960 ml water

160 g rolled oats

1 tablespoon light olive oil

1 large peach, peeled, pitted, and diced

¼ teaspoon salt

60 g toasted pecans

2 tablespoons maple syrup

1. Place water, oats, peach, oil, and salt in the pot. Stir well and close the lid. move slider to PRESSURE. Make sure the pressure release valve is in the SEAL position. The temperature will default to HIGH, which is the correct setting. Set time to 4 minutes. Select START/STOP to begin cooking. 2. When cooking is complete, turn the pressure relief valve to the VENT position for quick pressure relief. Move slider to the right to unlock the lid, then carefully open it. 3. Stir well. Serve oatmeal topped with pecans and maple syrup.

Per Serving: Calories 274; Fat 15.7g; Sodium 153mg; Carbs 43.72g; Fibre 9.1g; Sugar 10.89g; Protein 9.67g

Buckwheat Porridge with Mixed Berries

Prep Time: 15 minutes | Cook Time: 6 minutes | Serves: 4

♦ ♦ ♦ ♦ ♦ ♦

165 g buckwheat groats, rinsed and drained
720 ml water
65 g chopped pitted dates
1 tablespoon light olive oil
¼ teaspoon ground cinnamon
¼ teaspoon salt

½ teaspoon vanilla extract
120 g blueberries
120 g raspberries
120 g hulled and quartered strawberries
2 tablespoons balsamic vinegar

♦ ♦ ♦ ♦ ♦ ♦

1. Add the water, buckwheat, dates, cinnamon, oil, and salt to the pot and stir well. Close the lid and move slider to PRESSURE. Make sure the pressure release valve is in the SEAL position. The temperature will default to HIGH, which is the correct setting. Set time to 6 minutes. Select START/STOP to begin cooking. 2. When cooking is complete, naturally release the pressure for 20 minutes. Then turn the pressure relief valve to the VENT position for quick pressure relief. Move slider to AIR FRY/ STOVETOP to unlock the lid, then carefully open it. Stir in vanilla. 3. While buckwheat cooks, combine blueberries, strawberries, raspberries, and vinegar in a medium bowl. Stir well. Top porridge with berry mixture. Serve hot.

Per Serving: Calories 255; Fat 4.11g; Sodium 157mg; Carbs 55.57g; Fibre 6.6g; Sugar 40.98g; Protein 3.1g

Cheese Polenta with Eggs

Prep Time: 10 minutes | Cook Time: 9 minutes | Serves: 4

♦ ♦ ♦ ♦ ♦ ♦

175 g uncooked polenta (not instant)
946 ml water
1 tsp salt, plus more if needed
¼ tsp freshly ground black pepper, plus more if needed

1 tbsp (15 ml) extra-virgin olive oil
4 large eggs
3 tbsp (43 g) unsalted butter
2 tbsp (30 ml) heavy whipping cream
55g grated Parmesan cheese, plus more for topping

♦ ♦ ♦ ♦ ♦ ♦

1. Add the polenta, water, salt and pepper to the pot and stir until well combined. 2. Close the lid and move slider to PRESSURE. Make sure the pressure release valve is in the SEAL position. The temperature will default to HIGH, which is the correct setting. Set time to 9 minutes. Select START/STOP to begin cooking. 3. In the meantime, heat the olive oil in a small skillet over high heat. Once the oil is shimmering, crack the eggs into the hot oil. Fry the eggs for about 4 minutes, or until the white part is firm. 4. Once the timer beeps, turn the pressure relief valve to the VENT position for quick pressure relief. Move slider to the right to unlock the lid, then carefully open it. 5. Stir in the butter, cream and cheese. Taste the polenta and adjust the salt and pepper, if needed. 6. Transfer the polenta to four bowls and top each with a fried egg.

Per Serving: Calories 285; Fat 18.69g; Sodium 904mg; Carbs 23.25g; Fibre 2.4g; Sugar 17.68g; Protein 8.36g

Cheese Spinach Frittata

Prep Time: 15 minutes | Cook Time: 26 minutes | Serves: 4

❖ ❖ ❖ ❖ ❖ ❖

1 tablespoon olive oil
½ medium onion, peeled and chopped
½ medium red pepper , seeded and chopped
60 g chopped fresh baby spinach
240 ml water

120 g crumbled feta cheese
6 large eggs, beaten
60 g low-fat plain Greek yogurt
½ teaspoon salt
½ teaspoon ground black pepper

❖ ❖ ❖ ❖ ❖ ❖

1. Move slider to AIR FRY/STOVETOP. Select SEAR/SAUTÉ and set to 3. Select START/STOP to begin preheating. Allow unit to preheat for 5 minutes. After 5 minutes, heat the oil in the pot. Add onion and pepper , and cook until tender, about 8 minutes. 2. Add spinach and cook until wilted, about 3 minutes. Press START/STOP to turn off the SEAR/SAUTÉ function. Transfer vegetables to a medium bowl to cool. Wipe out the inner pot. 3. Add water to the pot. Then place the bottom layer of the Deluxe Reversible Rack in the lower position in the pot. Spray a baking dish that fits the pot with nonstick cooking spray. Drain excess liquid from spinach mixture, then add to dish with cheese. 4. In a separate medium bowl, whisk the eggs, yogurt, salt, and black pepper until well combined. Pour over vegetable and cheese mixture. Cover dish tightly with foil, then gently lower onto the rack. 5. Close the lid and move slider to PRESSURE. Make sure the pressure release valve is in the SEAL position. The temperature will default to HIGH, which is the correct setting. Set time to 15 minutes. Select START/STOP to begin cooking. 6. When cooking is complete, naturally release the pressure for 10 minutes. Then turn the pressure relief valve to the VENT position for quick pressure relief. Move slider to AIR FRY/ STOVETOP to unlock the lid, then carefully open it. 7. Let stand for 10 to15 minutes before carefully removing the dish from the pot. 8. Run a thin knife around the edge of the frittata and turn it out onto a serving platter. Serve warm.

Per Serving: Calories 234; Fat 18.45g; Sodium 779mg; Carbs 6.35g; Fibre 0.8g; Sugar 3.99g; Protein 10.95g

Banana Date Buckwheat Porridge

Prep Time: 10 minutes | Cook Time: 4 minutes | Serves: 4

❖ ❖ ❖ ❖ ❖ ❖

165 g buckwheat groats
360 ml unsweetened vanilla almond milk
240 ml water
1 large banana, mashed

5 pitted dates, chopped
¾ teaspoon ground cinnamon
¾ teaspoon pure vanilla extract

❖ ❖ ❖ ❖ ❖ ❖

1. Place the buckwheat groats, water, almond milk, dates, banana, cinnamon, and vanilla in the pot and stir. 2. Close the lid and move slider to PRESSURE. Make sure the pressure release valve is in the SEAL position. The temperature will default to HIGH, which is the correct setting. Set time to 4 minutes. Select START/STOP to begin cooking. 3. When cooking is complete, turn the pressure relief valve to the VENT position for quick pressure relief. Move slider to the right to unlock the lid, then carefully open it. 4. Allow the porridge to cool slightly before spooning into bowls to serve.

Per Serving: Calories 132; Fat 1.35g; Sodium 60mg; Carbs 29.23g; Fibre 3.4g; Sugar 15.9g; Protein 2.41g

Parmesan Tomato and Asparagus Frittata

Prep Time: 15 minutes | Cook Time: 15 minutes | Serves: 4

240 ml water
1 teaspoon olive oil
150 g halved cherry tomatoes
65 g cooked asparagus tips
25 g grated Parmesan cheese

6 large eggs
60 g low-fat plain Greek yogurt
½ teaspoon salt
½ teaspoon ground black pepper

1. Add water to the pot. Then place the bottom layer of the Deluxe Reversible Rack in the lower position in the pot. 2. Brush a baking dish that fits the pot with olive oil. Add asparagus, tomatoes, and cheese to the baking dish. 3. In a medium bowl, whisk the eggs, yogurt, salt, and pepper. Pour over vegetable and cheese mixture. Cover dish tightly with aluminum foil, then gently lower onto the rack in the pot. 4. Close the lid and move slider to PRESSURE. Make sure the pressure release valve is in the SEAL position. The temperature will default to HIGH, which is the correct setting. Set time to 15 minutes. Select START/STOP to begin cooking. 5. When cooking is complete, naturally release the pressure for 10 minutes. Then turn the pressure relief valve to the VENT position for quick pressure relief. Move slider to AIR FRY/ STOVETOP to unlock the lid, then carefully open it. 6. Let stand for 10–15 minutes before carefully removing the baking dish from the pot. 7. Run a thin knife around the edge of the frittata and turn it out onto a serving platter. Serve warm.

Per Serving: Calories 162; Fat 10.04g; Sodium 439mg; Carbs 10.7g; Fibre 1.7g; Sugar 6.73g; Protein 8.29g

Delicious Coconut Almond Granola

Prep Time: 10 minutes | Cook Time: 7 minutes | Serves: 8

120 g old fashioned rolled oats
60 g unsweetened shredded coconut
10 g monk fruit sweetener

⅛ teaspoon salt
180 g almond butter
60 ml coconut oil

1. In a medium bowl, combine the oats, coconut, sweetener, and salt. Stir to mix well. Add the almond butter and oil and mix until well combined. 2. Spray a 15 cm cake pan with nonstick cooking oil. Transfer the oat mixture to the pan. 3. Pour 240 ml of water to the pot of your pressure cooker. Then place the bottom layer of the Deluxe Reversible Rack in the lower position in the pot. Place the pan on the rack. 4. Close the lid and move slider to PRESSURE. Make sure the pressure release valve is in the SEAL position. The temperature will default to HIGH, which is the correct setting. Set time to 7 minutes. Select START/STOP to begin cooking. 5. When cooking is complete, turn the pressure relief valve to the VENT position for quick pressure relief. Move slider to the right to unlock the lid, then carefully open it. 6. Remove the pan from the pot and transfer the granola to a baking sheet to cool completely (at least 30 minutes) before serving.

Per Serving: Calories 270; Fat 21.12g; Sodium 109mg; Carbs 21.89g; Fibre 5.3g; Sugar 6.79g; Protein 8.08g

Cinnamon Banana Steel Cut Oats

Prep Time: 10 minutes | Cook Time: 4 minutes | Serves: 4

❖ ❖ ❖ ❖ ❖ ❖

160 g steel cut oats
600 ml water
600 ml unsweetened vanilla almond milk
3 medium bananas, thinly sliced

1½ teaspoons ground cinnamon
1 teaspoon pure vanilla extract
¼ teaspoon salt
4 tablespoons walnut pieces

❖ ❖ ❖ ❖ ❖ ❖

1. Add the steel cut oats, banana slices, almond milk, water, cinnamon, vanilla, and salt to the pot and stir to mix well. 2. Close the lid and move slider to PRESSURE. Make sure the pressure release valve is in the SEAL position. The temperature will default to HIGH, which is the correct setting. Set time to 4 minutes. Select START/STOP to begin cooking. 3. When cooking is complete, naturally release the pressure for 15 minutes. Then turn the pressure relief valve to the VENT position for quick pressure relief. Move slider to AIR FRY/ STOVETOP to unlock the lid, then carefully open it. 4. Serve the oatmeal in a bowl topped with 1 tablespoon walnut pieces for each serving.
Per Serving: Calories 305; Fat 9.8g; Sodium 246mg; Carbs 62.89g; Fibre 11.2g; Sugar 21.12g; Protein 11.64g

Savoury Spinach and Artichoke Egg Casserole

Prep Time: 10 minutes | Cook Time: 18 minutes | Serves: 8

❖ ❖ ❖ ❖ ❖ ❖

12 large eggs
60 ml water
120 g baby spinach, roughly chopped
1 can baby artichoke hearts, drained and roughly chopped

1 tablespoon chopped fresh chives
1 tablespoon fresh lemon juice
¾ teaspoon table salt
½ teaspoon black pepper
¼ teaspoon garlic salt

❖ ❖ ❖ ❖ ❖ ❖

1. Spray a 15 cm round pan with cooking spray. 2. whisk together the eggs and water in a medium bowl. 3. Stir in the artichokes, spinach, chives, table salt, pepper, lemon juice, and garlic salt. 4. Transfer the mixture to the prepared pan. 5. Pour 480 ml water into the pot and place the steam rack inside. Place the pa Deluxe Reversible Rack in the lower position in the pot. Place the pan on the rack. 6. Close the lid and move slider to PRESSURE. Make sure the pressure release valve is in the SEAL position. The temperature will default to HIGH, which is the correct setting. Set time to 18 minutes. Select START/STOP to begin cooking. 7. When cooking is complete, turn the pressure relief valve to the VENT position for quick pressure relief. Move slider to the right to unlock the lid, then carefully open it. 8. Remove egg casserole from pot and allow to cool 5 minutes before slicing and serving.
Per Serving: Calories 128; Fat 6.96g; Sodium 254mg; Carbs 9.42g; Fibre 2.8g; Sugar 0.8g; Protein 7.14g

Cider–Braised Lentils with Leeks & Apple

Prep Time: 15 minutes | Cook Time: 4-5 hours | Serves: 6

3 medium leeks, white and light green parts thinly sliced, rinsed and dried
4 tablespoons salted butter
2 medium garlic cloves, finely chopped
1½ teaspoons fresh thyme leaves, minced
1 medium Granny Smith apple, peeled, cored and finely chopped
Salt and ground black pepper
400 g lentils du Puy, rinsed and drained
720 ml apple cider
1 bunch chives, thinly sliced
1 to 2 tablespoons balsamic vinegar (optional)

1. Move slider to AIR FRY/STOVETOP. Select SEAR/SAUTÉ and set to 3. Select START/STOP to begin preheating. Allow unit to preheat for 5 minutes. After 5 minutes, add the butter and melt. Add the leeks and cook, stirring occasionally, until lightly browned, 5 to 7 minutes. Stir in the garlic, apple, thyme, 2 teaspoons salt and ¼ teaspoon pepper. Cook, stirring, until fragrant, about 30 seconds. 2. Add the lentils, cider and 480 ml water; stir to combine well, then distribute in an even layer. Press START/STOP to turn off the SEAR/SAUTÉ function. 3. Close the lid and move slider to PRESSURE. Make sure the pressure release valve is in the SEAL position. The temperature will default to HIGH, which is the correct setting. Set time to 8 minutes. Select START/STOP to begin cooking. 4. When cooking is complete, press START/STOP and naturally release the pressure for 10 minutes. Then turn the pressure relief valve to the VENT position for quick pressure relief. Move slider to AIR FRY/ STOVETOP to unlock the lid, then carefully open it. 5. Move slider to AIR FRY/STOVETOP. Select SEAR/SAUTÉ and set to Hi5. Select START/STOP to begin cooking. Bring the mixture to a boil. 6. Close the lid in place and select Slow Cook and set the temperature to Low. Set the cooking time for 4 to 5 hours; the lentils are done when they are fully tender but still hold their shape. Press START/ STOP, then carefully open the pot. 7. Stir in the chives and balsamic vinegar (if using), then taste and season with salt and pepper. Serve warm.

Per Serving: Calories 158; Fat 5.57g; Sodium 56mg; Carbs 26.28g; Fibre 3.5g; Sugar 10.87g; Protein 4.11g

Spicy Curried Chickpeas and Cucumbers Salad

Prep Time: 15 minutes | Cook Time: 0 minute | Serves: 6

◆◆◆◆◆◆

1 kg boiled chickpeas
1 small red onion, finely chopped
2 teaspoons curry powder
Salt and ground black pepper
60 g tamarind chutney
1½ tablespoons hot sauce (such as Tabasco), plus more as needed

3 tablespoons lime juice, plus lime wedges, to serve
2 tablespoons packed brown sugar
100 g fried wonton strips
1 English cucumber, quartered lengthwise and cut crosswise into 1 cm pieces
30 g lightly packed fresh coriander leaves

◆◆◆◆◆◆

1. In a big bowl, toss the chickpeas with the onion, 2 teaspoons salt, curry powder and 1 teaspoon pepper; set aside. 2. In a small bowl, mix together the chutney, lime juice, hot sauce and sugar, whisk until the sugar dissolves. Taste and season with more hot sauce, if desired. 3. Pour the chutney mixture over the chickpeas and stir. Toss in the wonton strips, cucumber and half the coriander. Taste and season with salt and pepper. Sprinkle with the remaining coriander. Serve with the lime wedges.

Per Serving: Calories 327; Fat 4.56g; Sodium 135mg; Carbs 56.98g; Fibre 13.9g; Sugar 14.84g; Protein 15.85g

Greek "Fried" Rice with Cheese and Eggs

Prep Time: 10 minutes | Cook Time: 5 minutes | Serves: 4

◆◆◆◆◆◆

200 g long-grain white rice
1 can diced tomatoes, including juice
60 ml water
1 teaspoon salt
2 large eggs, whisked

75 g peeled and seeded diced English cucumber
30 g crumbled feta cheese
40 g sliced Kalamata olives
10 g chopped fresh mint leaves

◆◆◆◆◆◆

1. Add the rice, water, tomatoes with juice, and salt in the pot. 2. Close the lid and move slider to PRESSURE. Make sure the pressure release valve is in the SEAL position. The temperature will default to HIGH, which is the correct setting. Set time to 3 minutes. Select START/STOP to begin cooking. 3. When cooking is complete, naturally release the pressure for 10 minutes. Then turn the pressure relief valve to the VENT position for quick pressure relief. Move slider to AIR FRY/ STOVETOP to unlock the lid, then carefully open it. 4. Make a well in the middle of the rice and add whisked eggs to the well. Stir eggs into rice and stir-fry 2 minutes. 5. Transfer rice mixture to a serving dish. Toss in cucumber, feta cheese, and olives. 6. Garnish with mint leaves and serve warm.

Per Serving: Calories 251; Fat 5.77g; Sodium 861mg; Carbs 42.4g; Fibre 3.1g; Sugar 3.46g; Protein 7.12g

Turmeric Yellow Split Pea & Carrot Soup

Prep Time: 15 minutes | Cook Time: 6½-7½ hours | Serves: 6

2 tablespoons coconut oil, preferably unrefined
1 large yellow onion, finely chopped
6 medium garlic cloves, finely chopped
1 teaspoon dried thyme
1 teaspoon ground allspice
1 habanero or Scotch bonnet chili, stemmed
1.5 L low-sodium chicken stock

270 g yellow split peas, rinsed and drained
3 medium carrots, peeled, halved lengthwise and thinly sliced
Salt and ground black pepper
1 tablespoon ground turmeric
10 g finely chopped fresh coriander
Lime wedges, to serve

1. Move slider to AIR FRY/STOVETOP. Select SEAR/SAUTÉ and set to Hi5. Select START/STOP to begin cooking. Add the oil and heat until shimmering. Add the onion and cook, stirring frequently, until softened and golden brown at the edges, 5 to 7 minutes. 2. Stir in the garlic, thyme and allspice, then cook until fragrant, about 30 seconds. Add the stock, chili, and split peas; stir to combine well, then distribute in an even layer. Press START/STOP to turn off the SEAR/SAUTÉ function. 3. Close the lid and move slider to PRESSURE. Make sure the pressure release valve is in the SEAL position. The temperature will default to HIGH, which is the correct setting. Set time to 18 minutes. Select START/STOP to begin cooking. 4. When cooking is complete, turn the pressure relief valve to the VENT position for quick pressure relief. Move slider to the right to unlock the lid, then carefully open it. 5. With the pot still on SEAR/SAUTÉ function and set to Hi5, bring the mixture to a boil. 6. Close the lid in place and select Slow Cook and set the temperature to Low. Set the cooking time for 6 to 7 hours; the soup is done when the split peas have completely broken down. Press START/STOP, then carefully open the pot. 7. Stir the split pea mixture, scraping the bottom of the pot, then stir in the carrots. 8. Select SEAR/SAUTÉ and set to Hi5, stirring occasionally, until the carrots are tender, about 5 minutes. Press START/STOP to turn off the SEAR/SAUTÉ function. 9. Let rest for 10 minutes, then whisk in the turmeric and coriander. Remove and discard the chili. 10. Taste and season with salt and pepper.

Per Serving: Calories 140; Fat 7.59g; Sodium 159mg; Carbs 14.09g; Fibre 2.3g; Sugar 4.69g; Protein 5.61g

Chickpea Yogurt Pita Salad with Mint

Prep Time: 10 minutes | Cook Time: 4 minutes | Serves: 6

✦ ✦ ✦ ✦ ✦ ✦

340 g Simple Chickpeas
1½ teaspoons ground cumin, divided
Salt and ground black pepper
240 g plain whole-milk yogurt
55 g tahini
2 medium garlic cloves, finely chopped

1 teaspoon lemon zest, plus 1 tablespoon lemon juice, grated
30 g pine nuts
3 tablespoons salted butter, cut into 3 pieces
120 g pita chips
45 g lightly packed fresh mint, torn if large

✦ ✦ ✦ ✦ ✦ ✦

1. In a medium bowl, mix the chickpeas with 1 teaspoon of cumin and 1 teaspoon salt. In a small bowl, mix together the yogurt, tahini, lemon zest and juice, garlic, ½ teaspoon salt and ¼ teaspoon pepper. 2. Move slider to AIR FRY/STOVETOP. Select SEAR/SAUTÉ and set to 3. Select START/STOP to begin cooking. 3. Toast the pine nuts in the pot, stirring often, until golden brown and fragrant, 3 to 4 minutes. Add the butter, the remaining ½ teaspoon cumin and ¼ teaspoon each salt and pepper, stir until the butter is melted. Press START/STOP to turn off the SEAR/SAUTÉ function. Set aside. 4. Place the pita chips in a shallow serving bowl, then scatter on the chickpeas. Spoon on the yogurt mixture, then top with mint and the pine-nut butter mixture.
Per Serving: Calories 478; Fat 19.43g; Sodium 167mg; Carbs 60.62g; Fibre 10.9g; Sugar 11.54g; Protein 20.02g

Cheese Mushroom Risotto

Prep Time: 15 minutes | Cook Time: 11 minutes | Serves: 4

✦ ✦ ✦ ✦ ✦ ✦

4 tablespoons olive oil
4 tablespoons butter, divided
1 medium yellow onion, peeled and diced
4 cloves garlic, minced
200 g sliced mushrooms
300 g arborio rice

960 ml vegetable stock
100 g grated Parmesan cheese
1 teaspoon dried parsley
½ teaspoon salt
¼ teaspoon black pepper

✦ ✦ ✦ ✦ ✦ ✦

1. Move slider to AIR FRY/STOVETOP. Select SEAR/SAUTÉ and set to 3. Select START/STOP to begin cooking. Heat oil and 2 tablespoons butter in the pot. Add onion and cook for 3 minutes. 2. Add garlic and cook for 30 seconds. 3. Stir in mushrooms and rice. Pour in stock and deglaze bottom of pot. Press START/STOP to turn off the SEAR/SAUTÉ function. 4. Close the lid and move slider to PRESSURE. Make sure the pressure release valve is in the SEAL position. The temperature will default to HIGH, which is the correct setting. Set time to 7 minutes. Select START/STOP to begin cooking. 5. When cooking is complete, turn the pressure relief valve to the VENT position for quick pressure relief. Move slider to the right to unlock the lid, then carefully open it. 6. Mix in remaining 2 tablespoons butter, Parmesan cheese, salt, dried parsley, and pepper. 7. Serve hot.
Per Serving: Calories 483; Fat 41.26g; Sodium 837mg; Carbs 29.26g; Fibre 9.9g; Sugar 1.68g; Protein 13.75g

Delicious Parmesan–Lemon Chicken Risotto

Prep Time: 15 minutes | Cook Time: 21 minutes | Serves: 8

4 tbsp (55 g) grass-fed butter or ghee, divided
455 g boneless, skinless chicken breast, cut into 2.5-cm cubes
1 medium yellow onion, diced
5 cloves garlic, finely chopped
120 ml dry white wine
2 tbsp (30 ml) fresh lemon juice
195 g uncooked arborio or other short-grain white rice

1 tsp sea salt
475 ml vegetable or chicken stock
60 ml heavy cream
75 g shredded Parmesan cheese, plus more for garnish
15 g finely chopped fresh flat-leaf parsley, plus more for garnish
Zest of 2 small lemons

1. Move slider to AIR FRY/STOVETOP. Select SEAR/SAUTÉ and set to 3. Select START/STOP to begin preheating. Allow unit to preheat for 5 minutes. After 5 minutes, add 2 tablespoons (28 g) butter to the pot. Once the fat has melted, add the chicken and sauté, stirring occasionally, for 5 to 7 minutes, or until the pink colour is gone. Transfer to a plate and set aside. 2. Add the onion and sauté, stirring occasionally, for 7 minutes, or until caramelised. Then, add the garlic and sauté for 1 minute, stirring occasionally. Add wine and lemon juice to deglaze the pot, scraping up any browned bits with a wooden spoon. 3. Add the rice, then give everything a stir to combine, stirring for 1 minute. Press START/STOP to turn off the SEAR/SAUTÉ function. 4. Add the stock, salt, and sautéed the chicken, give everything a quick stir. 5. Close the lid and move slider to PRESSURE. Make sure the pressure release valve is in the SEAL position. The temperature will default to HIGH, which is the correct setting. Set time to 6 minutes. Select START/STOP to begin cooking. 6. When cooking is complete, naturally release the pressure for 10 minutes. Then turn the pressure relief valve to the VENT position for quick pressure relief. Move slider to AIR FRY/ STOVETOP to unlock the lid, then carefully open it. 7. Add the cream, Parmesan, the remaining 2 tablespoons of butter, parsley and lemon zest, then quickly stir until the cream and Parmesan are fully mixed in. Allow the mixture to rest for 10 minutes. 8. Serve immediately, garnished with shredded Parmesan and chopped fresh flat-leaf parsley.

Per Serving: Calories 308; Fat 10.88g; Sodium 1045mg; Carbs 37.59g; Fibre 2.1g; Sugar 5.28g; Protein 14.64g

Turmeric Basmati Rice with Onion

Prep Time: 5 minutes | Cook Time: 9 minutes | Serves: 8

2 tablespoons unsalted butter
35 g peeled and diced yellow onion
400 g basmati rice

480 ml chicken stock
1 teaspoon ground turmeric
⅛ teaspoon salt

1. Move slider to AIR FRY/STOVETOP. Select SEAR/SAUTÉ and set to 3. Select START/STOP to begin cooking. Add butter to the pot and heat 30 seconds until melted. Add the onion and cook for 5 minutes until onions are translucent. 2. Add the remaining ingredients. Press START/STOP to turn off the SEAR/SAUTÉ function and close the lid. 3. Move slider to PRESSURE. Make sure the pressure release valve is in the SEAL position. The temperature will default to HIGH, which is the correct setting. Set time to 3 minutes. Select START/STOP to begin cooking. 4. When cooking is complete, naturally release the pressure for 5 minutes. Then turn the pressure relief valve to the VENT position for quick pressure relief. Move slider to AIR FRY/ STOVETOP to unlock the lid, then carefully open it. 5. Ladle rice into eight bowls and serve warm.

Per Serving: Calories 210; Fat 12.54g; Sodium 289mg; Carbs 15.59g; Fibre 6.3g; Sugar 0.4g; Protein 17.08g

Red Beans & Sausage Stew with Rice

Prep Time: 15 minutes | Cook Time: 12 minutes | Serves: 6

♦ ♦ ♦ ♦ ♦ ♦

380 g uncooked brown rice
590 ml water
1 tsp salt, plus a pinch and more to taste
1 tsp extra-virgin olive oil
340 g andouille sausage, sliced
2 yellow onions, diced
1 celery rib, diced
1 pepper , seeded and diced
5 cloves garlic, grated

1 tsp smoked paprika
¼ tsp freshly ground black pepper, plus more to taste
¼ to ½ tsp cayenne pepper
½ tsp dried basil
½ tsp dried oregano
2 (430 g) cans red kidney beans, drained and rinsed, divided
120 ml chicken stock
3 dried bay leaves

♦ ♦ ♦ ♦ ♦ ♦

1. Place the rice and water along with a pinch of salt in the pot, stir to mix well. 2. Close the lid and move slider to PRESSURE. Make sure the pressure release valve is in the SEAL position. The temperature will default to HIGH, which is the correct setting. Set time to 1 minute. Select START/STOP to begin cooking. 3. When cooking is complete, naturally release the pressure for 15 minutes. Then turn the pressure relief valve to the VENT position for quick pressure relief. Move slider to AIR FRY/ STOVETOP to unlock the lid, then carefully open it. 4. Fluff the rice with a fork and transfer the rice to a plate. Clean out the pot. 5. Add the olive oil to the pot. Move slider to AIR FRY/STOVETOP. Select SEAR/SAUTÉ and set to 3. Select START/STOP to begin cooking. Once the oil is shimmering, add the sausage and sauté for 3 minutes. 6. Stir in the onions, celery and pepper . Sauté for 2 minutes. 7. Press START/STOP, then stir in the garlic, paprika, cayenne, basil, oregano, the remaining salt, black pepper. 8. Puree 128 g of the kidney beans in a food processor until smooth. Add to the pot along with the remaining beans, stock and bay leaves. 9. Close the lid and move slider to PRESSURE. Make sure the pressure release valve is in the SEAL position. The temperature will default to HIGH, which is the correct setting. Set time to 5 minutes. Select START/STOP to begin cooking. 10. When the timer sounds, quick release the pressure. Open the lid and stir the sausage and beans. Add more salt and black pepper to taste, if needed. 11. Serve the beans and sausage over the brown rice.

Per Serving: Calories 483; Fat 17.68g; Sodium 943mg; Carbs 64.61g; Fibre 5.1g; Sugar 2.95g; Protein 19.42g

Herbed Black-Eyed Peas and Greens

Prep Time: 10 minutes | Cook Time: 13 minutes | Serves: 2

1 tablespoon oil
½ yellow onion, diced
2 garlic cloves, minced
240 ml chicken stock
225 g dried black-eyed peas
60 g chopped Swiss chard or kale

1½ teaspoons red pepper flakes
2 fresh thyme sprigs or ½ teaspoon dried thyme
½ tablespoon salt
¼ teaspoon freshly ground black pepper
1 tablespoon apple cider vinegar
1 to 2 teaspoons hot sauce (optional)

1. Move slider to AIR FRY/STOVETOP. Select SEAR/SAUTÉ and set to Lo1. Select START/STOP to begin preheating. Allow unit to preheat for 5 minutes. After 5 minutes, add the onion to the pot. Cook, stirring frequently, for 2 minutes, or until softened. Add the garlic and cook, stirring, until fragrant, about 1 minute. 2. Add the stock, peas, Swiss chard, thyme, red pepper flakes, salt, and pepper. Deglaze the pot by scraping all the flavourful brown bits up off the bottom of the pot with a wooden spoon, then mix well. Press START/STOP to turn off the SEAR/SAUTÉ function. 3. Close the lid and move slider to PRESSURE. Make sure the pressure release valve is in the SEAL position. The temperature will default to HIGH, which is the correct setting. Set time to 10 minutes. Select START/STOP to begin cooking. 4. When cooking is complete, quick release pressure for 10 minutes. Carefully open the lid. 5. Stir in the vinegar and hot sauce (if using). Adjust seasoning if desired. Serve.

Per Serving: Calories 208; Fat 8.78g; Sodium 1726mg; Carbs 25.66g; Fibre 5.3g; Sugar 12.89g; Protein 8.54g

Asian Quinoa and Carrot Salad

Prep Time: 15 minutes | Cook Time: 1 minute | Serves: 3

180 g uncooked quinoa, rinsed
355 ml water
½ tsp sea salt, plus more to taste
60 ml avocado oil or extra-virgin olive oil
2 tbsp (30 ml) rice vinegar
2 tsp (10 ml) sesame oil
2 tsp (10 ml) soy sauce or tamari

½ tsp garlic powder
3 tbsp (24 g) diced green onion
130 g diced or matchstick-cut carrot
150 g seeded and diced red or orange pepper
10 g chopped fresh coriander
35 g chopped almonds or peanuts (optional)

1. Combine the quinoa, water and salt in the pot. 2. Close the lid and move slider to PRESSURE. Make sure the pressure release valve is in the SEAL position. The temperature will default to HIGH, which is the correct setting. Set time to 1 minute. Select START/STOP to begin cooking. 3. When cooking is complete, naturally release the pressure for 15 minutes. Then turn the pressure relief valve to the VENT position for quick pressure relief. Move slider to AIR FRY/STOVETOP to unlock the lid, then carefully open it. 4. In the meantime, make the dressing: In a small bowl, mix together the avocado oil, sesame oil, vinegar, soy sauce and garlic powder. Stir well. 5. Once the quinoa is completely done cooking, transfer to a big bowl. Mix in the carrot, green onion, pepper and coriander. Toss with the dressing. 6. Serve right away or store in the fridge for up to 5 days. Garnish with almonds or peanuts (if using) before serving.

Per Serving: Calories 608; Fat 33.95g; Sodium 966mg; Carbs 63.93g; Fibre 9.1g; Sugar 4.95g; Protein 16.75g

Brown Rice with Stir-Fried Vegetables

Prep Time: 10 minutes | Cook Time: 15 minutes | Serves: 2

3 tablespoons sesame oil, divided, plus more for greasing
150 g long-grain brown rice
180 ml water, plus 3 tablespoons
Salt
1 tablespoon cornflour
2 garlic cloves, crushed
1½ teaspoons peeled minced fresh ginger, divided

90 g broccoli florets
60 g julienned carrots
110 g snow peas, trimmed
3 fresh shiitake mushrooms, sliced
40 g drained sliced water chestnuts
2 to 3 tablespoons low-sodium soy sauce
40 g chopped onion

1. Grease the inside of the pressure cooker pot with sesame oil. 2. Add the rice, water and salt to the pot. Close the lid and move slider to PRESSURE. 3. Make sure the pressure release valve is in the SEAL position. The temperature will default to HIGH, which is the correct setting. Set time to 15 minutes. Select START/STOP to begin cooking. 4. When cooking is complete, naturally release the pressure for 10 minutes. Then turn the pressure relief valve to the VENT position for quick pressure relief. Move slider to AIR FRY/ STOVETOP to unlock the lid, then carefully open it. 5. While the rice is cooking, prepare the vegetables. Mix together the cornflour, garlic, ½ teaspoon of ginger, and 2 tablespoons of sesame oil in a large bowl. Stir until well combined and the cornflour is dissolved. Add the broccoli, mushrooms, carrots, snow peas, and water chestnuts and toss to lightly coat. 6. In a wok over medium heat, heat the remaining 1 tablespoon of sesame oil. Turn the heat to medium-high and add the vegetables. Cook for 2 minutes, tossing constantly to prevent burning. 7. Stir in the soy sauce and remaining 3 tablespoons of water. Add the onion and remaining 1 teaspoon of ginger and season with salt. Cook, stirring constantly, until the vegetables are tender but still crisp, 1 to 2 minutes. 8. Divide the brown rice between two plates and top with the stir-fried vegetables.

Per Serving: Calories 503; Fat 22.74g; Sodium 779mg; Carbs 67.84g; Fibre 4.8g; Sugar 3.8g; Protein 8.53g

Cheese Beans Burritos

Prep Time: 20 minutes | Cook Time: 50 minutes | Serves: 2

1 tablespoon olive oil

2 tablespoons chopped red onion

½ jalapeño pepper, stemmed, seeded, and finely chopped

1 garlic clove, finely minced

90 g canned pinto beans, rinsed and drained

480 ml water

½ teaspoon ground cumin

Salt

Freshly ground black pepper

50 g shredded Cheddar cheese

4 (20 cm) flour tortillas

1. Preheat the oven to 175°C. Line a baking sheet with aluminum foil. 2. Move slider to AIR FRY/STOVETOP. Select SEAR/SAUTÉ and set to 3. Select START/STOP to begin preheating. Allow unit to preheat for 5 minutes. After 5 minutes, heat the olive oil. Add the onion, garlic and jalapeño and cook for 1 - 2 minutes, stirring often. 3. Add the beans, water, salt and pepper. Press START/STOP to turn off the SEAR/SAUTÉ function. 4. Close the lid and move slider to PRESSURE. Make sure the pressure release valve is in the SEAL position. The temperature will default to HIGH, which is the correct setting. Set time to 35 minutes. Select START/STOP to begin cooking. 5. When cooking is complete, naturally release the pressure for 10 minutes. Then turn the pressure relief valve to the VENT position for quick pressure relief. Move slider to AIR FRY/ STOVETOP to unlock the lid, then carefully open it. 6. Drain the beans, reserving 480 ml of the cooking liquid in a bowl. Using an immersion blender or potato masher, process or mash the beans to your desired consistency, adding some of the reserved cooking water if needed for a smoother purée. 7. Mix together the beans and Cheddar cheese in a medium bowl. 8. Lay out the tortillas on a work surface. Scoop about some of the bean mixture onto one tortilla just below centre. Fold the bottom edge of the tortilla up and over the filling. Fold the sides in, overlapping them to enclose the filling. 9. Place the Deluxe Reversible Rack in the lower position in the pot. 10. Roll up the tortilla from the bottom, then place seam-side down on the rack. Repeat with the remaining tortillas and filling. 11. Close the lid and Move slider to AIR FRY/STOVETOP. Select BAKE/ ROAST, setting temperature to 175°C, set the time to 12 minutes and press START/STOP to begin cooking. 12. Bake until heated through. Serve with white rice and fresh salsa.

Per Serving: Calories 627; Fat 22.58g; Sodium 1093mg; Carbs 80.73g; Fibre 10.2g; Sugar 4.83g; Protein 24.94g

Lentil Salad with Greens

Prep Time: 15 minutes | Cook Time: 5 minutes | Serves: 6

260 g green lentils
480 ml water
60 ml raw apple cider vinegar
2 tablespoons extra-virgin olive oil
1½ teaspoons fine sea salt
Freshly ground black pepper
1 tablespoon spicy brown mustard
1 tablespoon pure maple syrup

1 clove garlic, minced
2 small minced shallots
1 English cucumber
1 red pepper
20 g lightly packed chopped fresh flat-leaf parsley
90 g raisins
90 g sliced almonds
Leafy greens, like arugula, for serving

1. Place the lentils and water in the pot and close the lid. 2. Move slider to PRESSURE. Make sure the pressure release valve is in the SEAL position. The temperature will default to HIGH, which is the correct setting. Set time to 4 minutes. Select START/STOP to begin cooking. 3. When cooking is complete, naturally release the pressure for 10 minutes. Then turn the pressure relief valve to the VENT position for quick pressure relief. Move slider to AIR FRY/ STOVETOP to unlock the lid, then carefully open it. 4. While the lentils are cooking, mix together the vinegar, salt, olive oil, several grinds of pepper, the mustard, garlic, maple syrup, and shallots to make a dressing. 5. Dice the cucumber and add it to the bowl of dressing to marinate. Seed and dice the red pepper , then add it and parsley to the bowl of dressing to marinate. 6. Pour the cooked lentils into a fine-mesh sieve and rinse with cold water to quickly cool them off. Add the cooked lentils to the bowl with the dressing and vegetables and toss well to coat. Stir in the raisins and almonds, then chill in the fridge for 1 hour. 7. Once the salad is chilled, taste and adjust the seasoning as needed. Serve the lentil salad along with the leafy greens. 8. Store leftovers in an airtight container in the fridge for 5 days.

Per Serving: Calories 70; Fat 2.47g; Sodium 666mg; Carbs 10.85g; Fibre 1.3g; Sugar 4.26g; Protein 3.06g

Barley & Beans Taco Salad with Zesty Lime Vinaigrette

Prep Time: 15 minutes | Cook Time: 20 minutes | Serves: 6

180 g barley
240 ml water
1 teaspoon ground cumin
1 teaspoon chili powder
185 g prepared salsa
½ teaspoon fine sea salt
260 g cooked or canned black beans
2 romaine hearts, chopped

180 g shredded red cabbage
150 g cherry tomatoes, halved
60 g chopped green onions, tender white and green parts only
20 g chopped fresh coriander
50 g crumbled feta or shredded Cheddar cheese
Avocado slices, for garnish

Zesty Lime Vinaigrette:

60 ml extra-virgin olive oil
3 tablespoons raw apple cider vinegar
60 ml freshly squeezed lime juice
3 tablespoons pure maple syrup
1 clove garlic, minced

1 teaspoon ground cumin
⅛ teaspoon cayenne pepper
½ teaspoon fine sea salt
Freshly ground black pepper

1. Add the barley, water, chili powder, salsa, cumin, and salt to the pot and stir to combine. Close the lid and move slider to PRESSURE. Make sure the pressure release valve is in the SEAL position. The temperature will default to HIGH, which is the correct setting. Set time to 20 minutes. Select START/STOP to begin cooking. 2. When cooking is complete, naturally release the pressure for 10 minutes. Then turn the pressure relief valve to the VENT position for quick pressure relief. Move slider to AIR FRY/ STOVETOP to unlock the lid, then carefully open it. 3. While the barley is cooking, prepare the vinaigrette. In a pint-sized mason jar, mix together the olive oil, lime juice, maple syrup, vinegar, garlic, cayenne, cumin, salt, and several grinds of pepper. Screw on the lid and shake vigorously to combine. Set aside. 4. Stir in the black beans to create the taco "meat. " (If using canned beans, drain and rinse them first.) 5. To serve, place the romaine, tomatoes, cabbage, green onions, coriander, and barley and black bean mixture in a serving bowl. Drizzle the lime vinaigrette on top and sprinkle with the cheese and avocado slices, and serve right away.

Per Serving: Calories 372; Fat 13.02g; Sodium 714mg; Carbs 56.14g; Fibre 13.4g; Sugar 12.38g; Protein 11.67g

Spicy Lentil & Walnut Tacos

Prep Time: 15 minutes | Cook Time: 5 minutes | Serves: 6

185 g green or brown lentils
300 ml water
1 teaspoon ground cumin
1 teaspoon chili powder
1 yellow onion, chopped
One can fire-roasted tomatoes with green chiles

90 g walnut halves
Lettuce, tomatoes, green onions, and avocado, or your favourite taco toppings, for serving
1 teaspoon fine sea salt
12 taco shells, for serving

1. Add the lentils, water, chili powder and cumin to the pot. Stir well and ensure the lentils are covered in liquid, then sprinkle the onion and canned tomatoes (along with their juices) over the top, do not stir. 2. Close the lid and move slider to PRESSURE. Make sure the pressure release valve is in the SEAL position. The temperature will default to HIGH, which is the correct setting. Set time to 5 minutes. Select START/STOP to begin cooking. 3. Meanwhile, finely chop the walnuts, lettuce, green onions, fresh tomatoes, and avocado. 4. When the cooking cycle is complete, naturally release the pressure for 10 minutes. Then turn the pressure relief valve to the VENT position for quick pressure relief. Move slider to AIR FRY/ STOVETOP to unlock the lid, then carefully open it. 5. Use a fork to mash a lentil against the side of the pot to make sure it's tender. If the lentils aren't tender, secure the lid (be sure the sealing ring is properly seated in the lid) and cook at high pressure for 2 minutes more. 6. Let the pressure naturally release for 5 minutes before venting and opening the lid. 7. Stir in the salt and chopped walnuts. Taste and adjust the seasonings as needed. 8. To serve, spoon the taco "meat" into taco shells, and top with lettuce, tomato, green onion, and avocado. Store leftover taco "meat" in an airtight container in the fridge for 5 days.

Per Serving: Calories 253; Fat 14.63g; Sodium 804mg; Carbs 27.64g; Fibre 3.5g; Sugar 1.55g; Protein 4.7g

Lime Hummus

Prep Time: 10 minutes | Cook Time: 30 minutes | Serves: 6

Garnish:

1 Roma tomato, seeded and small-diced
1 tablespoon red onion, peeled and finely diced
2 tablespoons chopped fresh coriander
1 teaspoon lime juice

1 clove garlic, peeled and minced
⅛ teaspoon cayenne pepper
⅛ teaspoon salt

Hummus:

90 g dried chickpeas
480 ml water
1 tablespoon tahini paste
2 cloves garlic, peeled and minced
1 tablespoon lime juice

1 teaspoon lime zest
¼ teaspoon ground cumin
¼ teaspoon chili powder
¼ teaspoon salt
2 tablespoons olive oil

1. In small bowl, mix the garnish ingredients. Refrigerate covered until ready to use. 2. Add chickpeas and water to the pot. 3. Close the lid and move slider to PRESSURE. Make sure the pressure release valve is in the SEAL position. The temperature will default to HIGH, which is the correct setting. Set time to 30 minutes. Select START/ STOP to begin cooking. 4. When cooking is complete, naturally release the pressure for 5 minutes. Then turn the pressure relief valve to the VENT position for quick pressure relief. Move slider to AIR FRY/ STOVETOP to unlock the lid, then carefully open it. 5. Drain the pot and reserve water. 6. Transfer chickpeas to a food processor. Add the tahini paste, garlic, lime juice, lime zest, chili powder, cumin, salt, and olive oil. If consistency is too thick, slowly add reserved water, 1 tablespoon at a time. 7. Transfer the hummus to a serving dish. Garnish with tomato mixture and serve.

Per Serving: Calories 122; Fat 6.29g; Sodium 159mg; Carbs 13.41g; Fibre 2.5g; Sugar 3.26g; Protein 3.94g

Orange, Apple and Pear Compote

Prep Time: 20 minutes | Cook Time: 10 minutes | Serves: 8

5 medium apples, peeled and chopped
3 medium pears, chopped
1 medium orange, thinly sliced
60 g dried cranberries
105 g packed brown sugar
100 g maple syrup

80 ml butter, cubed
2 tbsp. lemon juice
2 tsp. ground cinnamon
1 tsp. ground ginger
5 tbsp. orange juice, divided
4 tsp. cornflour

1. Combine the first 10 ingredients in the pot. Stir in 2 tbsp. orange juice. 2. Close the lid and move slider to PRESSURE. Make sure the pressure release valve is in the SEAL position. The temperature will default to HIGH, which is the correct setting. Set time to 6 minutes. Select START/STOP to begin cooking. 3. When cooking is complete, naturally release the pressure for 10 minutes. Then turn the pressure relief valve to the VENT position for quick pressure relief. Move slider to AIR FRY/ STOVETOP to unlock the lid, then carefully open it. 4. Move slider to AIR FRY/STOVETOP. Select SEAR/SAUTÉ and set to 4. Select START/STOP to begin cooking. Bring the liquid to a boil. 5. Stir the cornflour and remaining orange juice in a small bowl, mix until smooth; gradually stir into fruit mixture. 6. Cook and stir until sauce is thickened, 1 to 2 minutes.

Per Serving: Calories 302; Fat 8.01g; Sodium 69mg; Carbs 61.08g; Fibre 6.1g; Sugar 46.38g; Protein 1.03g

Hot Sour Pepper Sauce

Prep Time: 15 minutes | Cook Time: 2 minutes | Serves: 8

300 – 400 g fresh hot red peppers, stems removed, halved
240 ml distilled white vinegar

60 ml apple cider vinegar
3 garlic cloves, smashed

1. Combine together the peppers, cider vinegar, white vinegar, and garlic in the pot. Close the lid and move slider to PRESSURE. Make sure the pressure release valve is in the SEAL position. The temperature will default to HIGH, which is the correct setting. Set time to 2 minutes. Select START/STOP to begin cooking. 2. When cooking is complete, turn the pressure relief valve to the VENT position for quick pressure relief. Move slider to the right to unlock the lid, then carefully open it. 3. Keep your face away from the steam, which, depending on the spiciness of the peppers, can burn your sinuses. Using an immersion blender, food processor, or blender, blend the sauce until smooth. Strain through a fine-mesh sieve and store in glass bottles or jars at room temperature for up to 6 months.

Per Serving: Calories 29; Fat 0.2g; Sodium 6mg; Carbs 5.27g; Fibre 0.7g; Sugar 3.13g; Protein 0.87g

Buffalo Cheese Chicken Dip

Prep Time: 10 minutes | Cook Time: 15 minutes | Serves: 6

360 ml water
225 g boneless, skinless chicken breast
200 g cream cheese, cut into cubes
150 g shredded Cheddar cheese, divided

120 ml ranch dressing
5 tablespoons butter
2 tablespoons Worcestershire sauce
1 tablespoon red wine vinegar

1. Pour water into the pot. Then place the bottom layer of the Deluxe Reversible Rack in the lower position in the pot. 2. In a metal bowl, mix together the chicken, cream cheese, 50 g Cheddar cheese, butter, Worcestershire, ranch dressing, and vinegar. 3. Cover the bowl with a paper towel and piece of foil, crimped around the edges. Create a foil sling and lower bowl onto the rack in the pot. 4. Close the lid and move slider to PRESSURE. Make sure the pressure release valve is in the SEAL position. The temperature will default to HIGH, which is the correct setting. Set time to 15 minutes. Select START/STOP to begin cooking. 5. When cooking is complete, naturally release the pressure for 10 minutes. Then turn the pressure relief valve to the VENT position for quick pressure relief. Move slider to AIR FRY/ STOVETOP to unlock the lid, then carefully open it. 6. Carefully lift bowl out of the pot with the foil sling. Remove paper towel and foil from bowl. 7. Remove chicken from bowl and shred with two forks. 8. While dip is still hot, mix in shredded chicken and remaining Cheddar cheese. Stir until combined and cheese is melted.
Per Serving: Calories 466; Fat 41.02g; Sodium 761mg; Carbs 11.86g; Fibre 0.6g; Sugar 4.94g; Protein 13.34g

Cheese Artichoke Dip

Prep Time: 5 minutes | Cook Time: 7 minutes | Serves: 6

1 can quartered artichoke hearts, drained
1 can mild diced green chilies
240 g mayonnaise
1 teaspoon paprika

½ teaspoon garlic powder
220 g shredded mozzarella cheese
100 g grated Parmesan cheese

1. Add the artichoke hearts, green chilies, paprika, mayonnaise, and garlic powder to the pot. 2. Close the lid and move slider to PRESSURE. Make sure the pressure release valve is in the SEAL position. The temperature will default to HIGH, which is the correct setting. Set time to 7 minutes. Select START/STOP to begin cooking. 3 When the timer beeps, quick release pressure and then unlock the lid. 4. Mix in cheeses and serve hot.
Per Serving: Calories 271; Fat 17.5g; Sodium 996mg; Carbs 9.03g; Fibre 3.1g; Sugar 1.22g; Protein 20.18g

Spicy Black Bean Dip

Prep Time: 15 minutes | Cook Time: 39 minutes | Serves: 6

1 tablespoon olive oil
1 small red onion, peeled and diced
3 cloves garlic, peeled and minced
185 g dried black beans, rinsed
360 ml chicken stock
2 teaspoons chili powder

2 teaspoons ground cumin
1 teaspoon salt
¼ teaspoon cayenne pepper
1 can diced green chiles, including juice
1 can diced tomatoes, including juice
120 g sour cream

1. Move slider to AIR FRY/STOVETOP. Select SEAR/SAUTÉ and set to Lo1. Select START/STOP to begin preheating. Allow unit to preheat for 5 minutes. After 5 minutes, heat the oil for 30 seconds. Add onion to the pot and sauté for 5 minutes until the onions are translucent. Add garlic. Heat for an additional minute. 2. Add black beans, chili powder, cumin, stock, salt, cayenne pepper, green chiles with juice, and tomatoes with juice to the pot and stir to combine. 3. Close the lid and move slider to PRESSURE. Make sure the pressure release valve is in the SEAL position. The temperature will default to HIGH, which is the correct setting. Set time to 30 minutes. Select START/STOP to begin cooking. 4. When cooking is complete, turn the pressure relief valve to the VENT position for quick pressure relief. Move slider to the right to unlock the lid, then carefully open it. 5. Use an immersion blender to blend the dip in the pot until smooth. With dip still in pot, press the SEAR/SAUTÉ button and set to 3, heat for 3 minutes, stirring several times. 6. Transfer the dip to a serving dish. Garnish with sour cream and serve.
Per Serving: Calories 278; Fat 9.45g; Sodium 817mg; Carbs 27.36g; Fibre 7.4g; Sugar 3.18g; Protein 21.94g

Classic Muddy Buddies

Prep Time: 15 minutes | Cook Time: 15 minutes | Serves: 6

480 ml water
105 g semisweet chocolate chips
105 g smooth peanut butter
55 g butter

½ teaspoon vanilla extract
160 g square rice cereal
100 g icingsugar

1. Pour water into the pot and press SEAR/SAUTÉ, set the heat to Hi5 and bring the water to a boil. 2. Place a large metal bowl on the top of the pot, so it is sitting partially inside pot. 3. Place chocolate chips, peanut butter, butter, and vanilla in the bowl, stir constantly until fully melted and smooth, about 15 minutes. 4. Pour in cereal and stir until fully coated. 5. Sprinkle icing sugar on top and mix until evenly coated. Press START/STOP to turn off the SEAR/SAUTÉ function. 6. Spread muddy buddies onto parchment-lined baking pan and let cool. 7. Store in an air-tight container at room temperature. Muddy Buddies can be stored up to three days.
Per Serving: Calories 437; Fat 27.39g; Sodium 198mg; Carbs 39.87g; Fibre 5.1g; Sugar 18.78g; Protein 10.04g

Spiced Red Pepper Hummus

Prep Time: 10 minutes | Cook Time: 30 minutes | Serves: 6

90 g dried chickpeas
480 ml water
150 g jarred roasted red peppers with liquid, chopped and divided
1 tablespoon tahini paste
2 cloves garlic, peeled and minced
1 tablespoon lemon juice

1 teaspoon lemon zest
¼ teaspoon ground cumin
¼ teaspoon smoked paprika
⅛ teaspoon cayenne pepper
¼ teaspoon salt
1 teaspoon sesame oil
1 tablespoon olive oil

1. Add chickpeas and water to the pot. Drain the liquid from jar of roasted peppers into pot. Set aside drained peppers. 2. Close the lid and move slider to PRESSURE. Make sure the pressure release valve is in the SEAL position. The temperature will default to HIGH, which is the correct setting. Set time to 30 minutes. Select START/STOP to begin cooking. 3. When cooking is complete, naturally release the pressure for 5 minutes. Then turn the pressure relief valve to the VENT position for quick pressure relief. Move slider to AIR FRY/ STOVETOP to unlock the lid, then carefully open it. 4. Drain the pot, reserving liquid in a small bowl. 5. Transfer chickpeas to a food processor. Add all but ¼ chopped red peppers, garlic, tahini paste, lemon juice, lemon zest, cumin, cayenne pepper, smoked paprika, salt, sesame oil, and olive oil. If consistency is too thick, slowly add reserved liquid, 1 tablespoon at a time. 6. Transfer the hummus to a serving dish. Garnish with remaining chopped roasted red peppers and serve.

Per Serving: Calories 108; Fat 4.82g; Sodium 423mg; Carbs 13.27g; Fibre 2.5g; Sugar 2.8g; Protein 3.93g

Lime Barbacoa Bella Burrito Bowls

Prep Time: 5 minutes | Cook Time: 10 minutes | Serves: 2

480 g Adobo Barbacoa sauce
200 g portobello mushrooms, chopped
Juice of ½ lime
1 bay leaf

Salt
190 g cooked white rice
90 g cooked black beans
50 g shredded Cheddar cheese

1. Pour the barbacoa sauce into the pot and add the mushrooms, lime juice, and bay leaf. Stir together. 2. Close the lid and cook on high pressure for 5 minutes, then allow the pressure to naturally release for 10 minutes. Then turn the pressure relief valve to the VENT position for quick pressure relief. Move slider to AIR FRY/ STOVETOP to unlock the lid, then carefully open it. 3. Move slider to AIR FRY/STOVETOP. Select SEAR/SAUTÉ and set to 3. Select START/STOP to begin cooking. Remove the bay leaf, then allow the contents to simmer for about 5 minutes, or until thickened. Season to taste with salt. 4. Serve in bowls over the cooked rice and black beans, topped with the Cheddar cheese and, as desired, shredded lettuce, pico de gallo, guacamole, and sour cream.

Per Serving: Calories 663; Fat 11.55g; Sodium 1964mg; Carbs 131.35g; Fibre 21.8g; Sugar 13.04g; Protein 27.13g

Chili Pork Picadillo Lettuce Wraps

Prep Time: 30 minutes | Cook Time: 30 minutes | Serves: 4

✦ ✦ ✦ ✦ ✦ ✦

3 garlic cloves, minced
1 tbsp. chili powder
1 tsp. salt
½ tsp. pumpkin pie spice
½ tsp. ground cumin
½ tsp. pepper
2 pork tenderloins
1 large onion, chopped

1 small sweet red pepper, chopped
1 can diced tomatoes and green chilies, undrained
1 small Granny Smith apple, peeled and chopped
240 ml water
60 g golden raisins
55 g chopped pimiento-stuffed olives
24 Bibb or Boston lettuce leaves
30 g slivered almonds, toasted

✦ ✦ ✦ ✦ ✦ ✦

1. Mix garlic and seasonings in a small bowl. Rub this mixture over the pork and transfer the pork to the pot. Add the onion, apple, tomatoes, sweet pepper and water. 2. Close the lid and move slider to PRESSURE. Make sure the pressure release valve is in the SEAL position. The temperature will default to HIGH, which is the correct setting. Set time to 25 minutes. Select START/STOP to begin cooking. 3. When cooking is complete, naturally release the pressure for 10 minutes. Then turn the pressure relief valve to the VENT position for quick pressure relief. Move slider to AIR FRY/ STOVETOP to unlock the lid, then carefully open it. 4. Remove the pork and let cool slightly. Shred meat into bite-size pieces; return to the pot. 5. Move slider to AIR FRY/STOVETOP. Select SEAR/SAUTÉ and set to Lo1. Select START/STOP to begin cooking. Stir in raisins and olives; heat through about 5 minutes. 6. Serve in lettuce leaves; sprinkle with slivered almonds.

Per Serving: Calories 515; Fat 11.23g; Sodium 1218mg; Carbs 39.62g; Fibre 7.9g; Sugar 21.61g; Protein 66.53g

Cheddar Cream Bacon Beer Dip

Prep Time: 15 minutes | Cook Time: 10 minutes | Serves: 6

✦ ✦ ✦ ✦ ✦ ✦

450 g cream cheese, softened
60 g sour cream
1½ tbsp. Dijon mustard
1 tsp. garlic powder
240 ml beer or nonalcoholic beer

455 g bacon strips, cooked and crumbled
200 g shredded cheddar cheese
60 g heavy whipping cream
1 green onion, thinly sliced
Soft pretzel bites

✦ ✦ ✦ ✦ ✦ ✦

1. Combine the cream cheese, sour cream, mustard and garlic powder in the pot, stir until smooth. Stir in beer, crumbled bacon, reserving 2 tbsp. 2. Close the lid and move slider to PRESSURE. Make sure the pressure release valve is in the SEAL position. The temperature will default to HIGH, which is the correct setting. Set time to 5 minutes. Select START/STOP to begin cooking. 3. When cooking is complete, turn the pressure relief valve to the VENT position for quick pressure relief. Move slider to the right to unlock the lid, then carefully open it. 4. Move slider to AIR FRY/STOVETOP. Select SEAR/SAUTÉ and set to 3. Select START/STOP to begin cooking. Stir in the cheese and heavy cream. Cook and stir until mixture has thickened, 3 to 4 minutes. 5. Transfer to a serving dish. Sprinkle with onion and reserved bacon. Serve with pretzel bites.

Per Serving: Calories 755; Fat 62.98g; Sodium 1580mg; Carbs 24.5g; Fibre 2.5g; Sugar 3.42g; Protein 25.61g

Maple Barbecue Sauce

Prep Time: 15 minutes | Cook Time: 9 minutes | Serves: 12

2 tablespoons minced onion
2 garlic cloves, minced
1 teaspoon smoked paprika
1 teaspoon ground allspice
240 ml water

1 can no-salt-added tomato sauce
55 g maple syrup
2 tablespoons stone-ground mustard
2 tablespoons apple cider vinegar
½ teaspoon salt (optional)

1. Move slider to AIR FRY/STOVETOP. Select SEAR/SAUTÉ and set to 3. Select START/STOP to begin preheating. Allow unit to preheat for 2 minutes. After 2 minutes, sauté the onion for 2 minutes, adding some water as needed to prevent sticking, until slightly browned. Add the garlic, paprika, and allspice and stir for 30 seconds, until fragrant. Stir in the water, scraping up any browned bits from the bottom of the pot. Add the tomato sauce, maple syrup, mustard, vinegar, and salt (if using). Whisk to combine. Press START/STOP to turn off the SEAR/SAUTÉ function. 2. Close the lid and move slider to PRESSURE. Make sure the pressure release valve is in the SEAL position. The temperature will default to HIGH, which is the correct setting. Set time to 4 minutes. Select START/STOP to begin cooking. 3. When the timer beeps, quick-release the pressure and carefully open the lid. If the sauce is not thick enough for your taste, select the SEAR/SAUTÉ function and allow the sauce to reduce, stirring frequently, until it reaches your desired consistency. 4. Store in the fridge for up to 4 weeks in a covered container.

Per Serving: Calories 31; Fat 0.52g; Sodium 102mg; Carbs 6.56g; Fibre 1g; Sugar 5.1g; Protein 0.66g

Savoury Tomato Ketchup

Prep Time: 15 minutes | Cook Time: 20 minutes | Serves: 16

900 g plum tomatoes, roughly chopped
5 pitted dates
6 tablespoons distilled white vinegar
1 tablespoon gluten-free vegan Worcestershire sauce
1 tablespoon paprika
1 teaspoon onion powder
1 teaspoon salt (optional)

½ teaspoon mustard powder
¼ teaspoon celery seed
¼ teaspoon garlic powder
Pinch of ground cloves
2 tablespoons water
1 tablespoon cornflour

1. Mix together the tomatoes, dates, Worcestershire sauce, paprika, vinegar, onion powder, salt (if using), celery seed, garlic powder, mustard powder, and cloves in the pot. Using a potato masher, mash the tomatoes until they have released much of their liquid. 2. Close the lid and move slider to PRESSURE. Make sure the pressure release valve is in the SEAL position. The temperature will default to HIGH, which is the correct setting. Set time to 5 minutes. Select START/STOP to begin cooking. 3. When cooking is complete, turn the pressure relief valve to the VENT position for quick pressure relief. Move slider to the right to unlock the lid, then carefully open it. 4. Move slider to AIR FRY/STOVETOP. Select SEAR/SAUTÉ and set to Lo1. Select START/STOP to begin cooking. Simmer about 10 minutes, until reduced, stirring frequently. 5. In a small bowl, mix together the water and cornflour and add to the simmering ketchup, stirring until thickened, 2 to 4 minutes more. Strain the ketchup through a fine-mesh sieve. The ketchup will thicken as it cools. Store in the fridge for up to 6 months in a covered container.

Per Serving: Calories 63; Fat 0.15g; Sodium 167mg; Carbs 15.92g; Fibre 0.9g; Sugar 14.18g; Protein 0.38g

Mini Balsamic Mozzarella Meatballs

Prep Time: 20 minutes | Cook Time: 30 minutes | Serves: 5

225 g minced beef
225 g minced pork
2 large eggs
1 tablespoon Italian seasoning
1 teaspoon garlic powder
1 teaspoon celery seed
½ teaspoon onion powder
½ teaspoon smoked paprika
40 g old-fashioned oats

20 mini mozzarella balls
3 tablespoons avocado oil, divided
1 can diced tomatoes, drained
480 ml water
20 fresh basil leaves
5 pearl tomatoes, sliced into 20 slices
1 tablespoon olive oil
1 tablespoon balsamic vinegar

1. In a medium bowl, mix together the beef, pork, eggs, garlic powder, oats, celery seed, onion powder, Italian seasoning and smoked paprika. Form this mixture into 20 meatballs. Then, press 1 mozzarella ball into the middle of each of the meatballs. 2. Move slider to AIR FRY/STOVETOP. Select SEAR/SAUTÉ and set to Lo1. Select START/STOP to begin preheating. Allow unit to preheat for 5 minutes. After 5 minutes, heat 2 tablespoons avocado oil. Place 10 meatballs around the edge of the pot. Sear all sides of the meatballs for 3 to 4 minutes. 3. Remove meatballs from the pot and set aside. Add the remaining 1 tablespoon avocado oil and repeat to cook the remaining meatballs. 4. Discard extra juice and oil. Add seared meatballs to a metal dish that fits the pot. Add drained diced tomatoes. 5. Add 480 ml water to the pot. Then place the bottom layer of the Deluxe Reversible Rack in the lower position in the pot. 6. Place the metal dish on top of the rack. 7. Close the lid and move slider to PRESSURE. Make sure the pressure release valve is in the SEAL position. The temperature will default to HIGH, which is the correct setting. Set time to 20 minutes. Select START/STOP to begin cooking. 8. When cooking is complete, naturally release the pressure for 10 minutes. Then turn the pressure relief valve to the VENT position for quick pressure relief. Move slider to AIR FRY/ STOVETOP to unlock the lid, then carefully open it. 9. Skewer a meatball, a basil leaf, and a tomato slice on a toothpick. Repeat 20 times. Drizzle skewered meatballs with olive oil and balsamic vinegar. Serve immediately.

Per Serving: Calories 504; Fat 30.72g; Sodium 717mg; Carbs 14.59g; Fibre 4.8g; Sugar 4.36g; Protein 44.99g

Lentil Celery Pâté

Prep Time: 5 minutes | Cook Time: 20 minutes | Serves: 10

2 tablespoons olive oil
1 small onion, peeled and diced
1 celery stalk, diced
3 cloves garlic, minced
360 g dried lentils
960 ml water

1 teaspoon red wine vinegar
2 tablespoons tomato paste
1 teaspoon ground coriander
1 teaspoon ground cumin
1 teaspoon sea salt
1 teaspoon ground black pepper

1. Move slider to AIR FRY/STOVETOP. Select SEAR/SAUTÉ and set to Lo1. Select START/STOP to begin preheating. Allow unit to preheat for 5 minutes. After 5 minutes, heat the oil and add onions and celery. Sauté for 3 to 5 minutes until the onions are translucent. Add garlic. Cook for an additional minute. Add remaining ingredients. 2. Close the lid and move slider to PRESSURE. Make sure the pressure release valve is in the SEAL position. The temperature will default to HIGH, which is the correct setting. Set time to 15 minutes. Select START/STOP to begin cooking. 3. When cooking is complete, naturally release the pressure for 10 minutes. Then turn the pressure relief valve to the VENT position for quick pressure relief. Move slider to AIR FRY/ STOVETOP to unlock the lid, then carefully open it. 4. Transfer ingredients to a blender or food processor and process until smooth. Spoon into a serving bowl and serve.

Per Serving: Calories 49; Fat 2.87g; Sodium 240mg; Carbs 5.3g; Fibre 0.6g; Sugar 0.73g; Protein 1.73g

Lemon Potato Puree

Prep Time: 15 minutes | Cook Time: 7 minutes | Serves: 10

3 medium yellow potatoes, cut into 2.5 cm chunks
1 large carrot, cut into 2.5 cm chunks
480 ml water
25 g nutritional yeast
2 tablespoons freshly squeezed lemon juice

2 teaspoons chickpea miso paste
½ teaspoon onion powder
½ teaspoon garlic powder
½ teaspoon mustard powder
¼ teaspoon ground turmeric

1. Add the potatoes, carrot, and water to the pot. Close the lid and move slider to PRESSURE. Make sure the pressure release valve is in the SEAL position. The temperature will default to HIGH, which is the correct setting. Set time to 7 minutes. Select START/STOP to begin cooking. 2. When cooking is complete, naturally release the pressure for 10 minutes. Then turn the pressure relief valve to the VENT position for quick pressure relief. Move slider to AIR FRY/ STOVETOP to unlock the lid, then carefully open it. 3. Using a slotted spoon, remove the potatoes and carrots to a blender, then add 120 ml of the cooking water along with the nutritional yeast, miso, onion powder, lemon juice, mustard powder, garlic powder, and turmeric. Blend until smooth and creamy, adding more cooking water as necessary to thin. Store in the fridge for up to 4 days in a covered container.

Per Serving: Calories 106; Fat 0.27g; Sodium 272mg; Carbs 22.29g; Fibre 3.2g; Sugar 1.48g; Protein 4.22g

Delicious Lemon Garlic Chicken Wings

Prep Time: 10 minutes | Cook Time: 15 minutes | Serves: 6

◆ ◆ ◆ ◆ ◆ ◆

80 ml olive oil
60 ml fresh lemon juice
1 tablespoon lemon zest
4 garlic cloves, minced
¼ teaspoon sea salt

Pinch of cayenne pepper
900 g chicken wings
240 ml chicken stock
10 g chopped parsley

◆ ◆ ◆ ◆ ◆ ◆

1. Whisk together olive oil, lemon juice, lemon zest, garlic, salt, and cayenne pepper in a large bowl. 2. If you buy chicken wings that are connected, cut them at the joint to separate. Add the chicken wings to lemon juice mixture and toss well. Refrigerate covered for 1 hour. 3. Add chicken stock to the pot. lace the Cook & Crisp Basket in the lower position in the pot. 4. Place the chicken wings on the basket. Stand up wings if desired so as to not overcrowd them on top of each other. 5. Close the lid and move slider to PRESSURE. Make sure the pressure release valve is in the SEAL position. The temperature will default to HIGH, which is the correct setting. Set time to 10 minutes. Select START/STOP to begin cooking. 6. When cooking is complete, naturally release the pressure for 5 minutes. Then turn the pressure relief valve to the VENT position for quick pressure relief. 7. Move slider to AIR FRY/STOVETOP. Select BROIL and press START/STOP to begin cooking. Broil for 3–5 minutes until browned. Transfer to a serving plate and garnish with chopped parsley.

Per Serving: Calories 366; Fat 20.12g; Sodium 386mg; Carbs 2.17g; Fibre 0.2g; Sugar 0.39g; Protein 42.14g

Traditional Salsa Verde

Prep Time: 5 minutes | Cook Time: 2 minutes | Serves: 8

◆ ◆ ◆ ◆ ◆ ◆

455 g tomatillos, outer husks removed
2 small jalapeños, seeded and chopped
1 small onion, peeled and diced
15 g chopped fresh coriander

1 teaspoon ground coriander
2 teaspoons sea salt
360 ml water

◆ ◆ ◆ ◆ ◆ ◆

1. Cut the tomatillos in half and place in the pot. Add enough water to cover the tomatillos. 2. Close the lid and move slider to PRESSURE. Make sure the pressure release valve is in the SEAL position. The temperature will default to HIGH, which is the correct setting. Set time to 2 minutes. Select START/STOP to begin cooking. 3. When cooking is complete, turn the pressure relief valve to the VENT position for quick pressure relief. Move slider to the right to unlock the lid, then carefully open it. 4. Drain the pot. Add tomatillos, onion, jalapeños, coriander, coriander, sea salt, and 360 ml water to a food processor or blender. Pulse until well combined, about 1 to 2 minutes. 5. Transfer to a serving dish and chill covered before serving.

Per Serving: Calories 104; Fat 4.93g; Sodium 605mg; Carbs 4.17g; Fibre 1.3g; Sugar 2.61g; Protein 10.71g

Chapter 4   Vegetables and Sides Recipes

Creamy Cheese Mushroom Risotto

Prep Time: 15 minutes | Cook Time: 15 minutes | Serves: 8

4 tbsp (55 g) grass-fed butter or ghee, divided
1 medium yellow onion, diced
680 g mushrooms, woody ends removed, thinly sliced
5 cloves garlic, finely chopped
120 ml dry white wine
195 g uncooked arborio or other short-grain white rice
1 large celery rib with leaves, thinly sliced

1 tsp sea salt
475 ml chicken or vegetable stock
60 ml heavy cream
40 g shredded Parmesan cheese, plus more for garnish
15 g finely chopped fresh flat-leaf parsley, plus more for garnish
1 tsp finely chopped fresh thyme leaves

1. Place 2 tablespoons butter in the pot. Move slider to AIR FRY/STOVETOP. Select SEAR/SAUTÉ and set to 3. Select START/STOP to begin cooking. and press sauté. Once the butter has melted, add the onion and mushrooms and sauté, stirring occasionally, for 7 minutes, or until caramelized. 2. Then, add the garlic and sauté for 1 minute, stirring occasionally. Add the wine and deglaze the pot, scraping up any browned bits with a wooden spoon. 3. Add the rice, then give everything a stir to combine, stirring for 1 minute. Press START/STOP to turn off the SEAR/ SAUTÉ function. 4. Add the celery, salt and stock, then give everything a quick stir. 5. Close the lid and move slider to PRESSURE. Make sure the pressure release valve is in the SEAL position. The temperature will default to HIGH, which is the correct setting. Set time to 6 minutes. Select START/STOP to begin cooking. 6. When cooking is complete, naturally release the pressure for 10 minutes. Then turn the pressure relief valve to the VENT position for quick pressure relief. Move slider to AIR FRY/ STOVETOP to unlock the lid, then carefully open it. 7. Add the cream, the remaining 2 tablespoons of butter, Parmesan, thyme and parsley, then quickly stir until the cream and Parmesan are fully mixed in. Allow the mixture to rest for 10 minutes. 8. Serve right away, garnished with shredded Parmesan and chopped fresh flat-leaf parsley.

Per Serving: Calories 484; Fat 11.92g; Sodium 855mg; Carbs 88.59g; Fibre 11.2g; Sugar 3.83g; Protein 16.69g

Loaded Mashed Cheese Potatoes

Prep Time: 15 minutes | Cook Time: 10 minutes | Serves: 6

240 ml water

5 medium russet potatoes, peeled and cut into 5-cm cubes

4 tbsp (55 g) grass-fed butter

230 g sour cream

120 ml milk or heavy cream

1 tsp sea salt

115 g shredded cheddar cheese

80 g shredded Italian cheese blend (equal parts provolone, Romano and Parmesan)

170 g precooked crispy bacon or turkey bacon, crumbled

1 spring onion, white and light green parts only, sliced

1. Pour the water into the pot and place the bottom layer of the Deluxe Reversible Rack in the lower position in the pot. 2. Layer the potatoes on the rack. 3. Close the lid and move slider to PRESSURE. Make sure the pressure release valve is in the SEAL position. The temperature will default to HIGH, which is the correct setting. Set time to 10 minutes. Select START/STOP to begin cooking. 4. When cooking is complete, turn the pressure relief valve to the VENT position for quick pressure relief. Move slider to the right to unlock the lid, then carefully open it. 5. Carefully remove the potatoes and the rack, setting the potatoes aside. Pour out and discard the water that remains in the pot, then return the potatoes to the pot; alternatively, transfer the potatoes to a large bowl. 6. Add the butter, allowing it to melt over the potatoes. Once the butter has melted, add the sour cream, milk and salt, then use a potato masher to start mixing everything together—do not overmix, just mash until there are no more lumps. 7. Gently fold in the cheeses, 115 g of the crumbled crispy bacon bits and the spring onions until all of the cheese has melted into the hot potatoes and everything is incorporated; do not overmix. 8. Serve immediately, garnished with the remaining 2 ounces (55 g) of crumbled crispy bacon bits.

Per Serving: Calories 674; Fat 35.73g; Sodium 1225mg; Carbs 62.35g; Fibre 4.7g; Sugar 2.34g; Protein 29.33g

Simple Artichokes with Lemon–Garlic Butter

Prep Time: 15 minutes | Cook Time: 13 minutes | Serves: 4

4 medium to large globe artichokes

Juice of 1 lemon, divided

240 ml water

1 tsp Dijon mustard

1 clove garlic

¼ tsp sea salt, plus more to taste

4 tbsp (55 g) unsalted butter or ghee, melted

1. Remove the outer leaves of the artichokes, trim about 1.3 cm from the top and remove the stem so each artichoke can sit upright. Brush each artichoke with lemon juice, reserve the remaining lemon juice and set aside. 2. Pour the water into the pot and place the bottom layer of the Deluxe Reversible Rack in the lower position in the pot. Place the artichokes, stem side down, on the rack so they sit upright. 3. Close the lid and move slider to PRESSURE. Make sure the pressure release valve is in the SEAL position. The temperature will default to HIGH, which is the correct setting. Set time to 13 minutes. Select START/STOP to begin cooking. 4. In the meantime, prepare the lemon-garlic butter. In a small bowl, stir the Dijon, garlic, remaining lemon juice and salt into the butter. 5. Serve warm with the lemon-garlic butter on the side for dipping. Sprinkle with additional salt to taste.

Per Serving: Calories 178; Fat 10.9g; Sodium 621mg; Carbs 19.33g; Fibre 13.1g; Sugar 1.83g; Protein 4.99g

Flavourful Citrus Beetroots

Prep Time: 15 minutes | Cook Time: 23 minutes | Serves: 6

240 ml water

5 medium beetroot, about 5 cm in diameter, leaves removed

2 tbsp (28 g) grass-fed butter, ghee or avocado oil

¾ tsp sea salt

Zest of 1 orange

Juice of 1 orange

1. Pour the water into the pot and place the bottom layer of the Deluxe Reversible Rack in the lower position in the pot. Place the beetroot on the rack. 2. Close the lid and move slider to PRESSURE. Make sure the pressure release valve is in the SEAL position. The temperature will default to HIGH, which is the correct setting. Set time to 20 minutes. Select START/STOP to begin cooking. 3. Once the timer sounds, naturally release the pressure for 15 minutes. Then turn the pressure relief valve to the VENT position for quick pressure relief. Move slider to AIR FRY/ STOVETOP to unlock the lid, then carefully open it. 4. Carefully remove the beetroot and rack, setting the beetroot aside on a cutting board. Pour out and discard the water that remains in the pot. 5. Slice off the tops of the beetroot and carefully slide or cut off the skin—it should come off very easily—then discard the tops and peeled-off skin. Using a sharp knife, slice the beetroot into round slices about 6 mm thick. 6. Add butter to the pot. Move slider to AIR FRY/STOVETOP. Select SEAR/SAUTÉ and set to 3. Select START/STOP to begin cooking. Once the butter has melted, add the beetroot back to the pot along with the salt and the orange zest and juice, gently stirring occasionally for 2 minutes to warm the citrus. Press START/ STOP to turn off the SEAR/SAUTÉ function. 7. Serve immediately.

Per Serving: Calories 80; Fat 4.03g; Sodium 375mg; Carbs 10.64g; Fibre 3.1g; Sugar 4.62g; Protein 1.48g

Ginger–Garlic Bok Choy

Prep Time: 15 minutes | Cook Time: 6 minutes | Serves: 4

3 tbsp (43 g) grass-fed butter or ghee

1 2-cm piece fresh ginger, peeled and finely minced

3 cloves garlic, minced

¾ tsp sea salt

3 tbsp (45 ml) coconut aminos

120 ml filtered water

7 baby bok choy, cut in half down the middle

1 spring onion, white and light green parts only, sliced on a bias

1 tsp toasted sesame oil, for garnish

1. Add butter to the pot. Move slider to AIR FRY/STOVETOP. Select SEAR/SAUTÉ and set to 3. Select START/STOP to begin cooking. Once the butter has melted, add the ginger and garlic and sauté for 2 minutes, stirring occasionally. Press START/STOP to turn off the SEAR/SAUTÉ function. 2. Add the salt, coconut aminos and water to the pot, then add the bok choy and spring onion and stir gently. 3. Close the lid and move slider to PRESSURE. Make sure the pressure release valve is in the SEAL position. The temperature will default to HIGH, which is the correct setting. Set time to 3 minutes. Select START/STOP to begin cooking. 4. Once the timer sounds, naturally release the pressure for 5 minutes. Then turn the pressure relief valve to the VENT position for quick pressure relief. Move slider to AIR FRY/ STOVETOP to unlock the lid, then carefully open it. 5. Serve immediately, drizzled with the toasted sesame oil.

Per Serving: Calories 187; Fat 12.62g; Sodium 501mg; Carbs 2.15g; Fibre 0.7g; Sugar 0.74g; Protein 16.11g

Healthy Ratatouille

Prep Time: 25 minutes | Cook Time: 23 minutes | Serves: 2

◆ ◆ ◆ ◆ ◆ ◆

1 small aubergine, chopped
Salt
2 tablespoons oil, divided
1 small onion, chopped
1 garlic clove, minced
1 tablespoon mashed roasted garlic
1 courgette, chopped

1 green pepper , seeded and chopped
60 ml dry white wine
120 ml vegetable stock or water
2 basil leaves
½ teaspoon herbes de Provence
Freshly ground black pepper
1 can crushed tomatoes with their juices

◆ ◆ ◆ ◆ ◆ ◆

1. In a colander set over a medium bowl, sprinkle salt on the aubergine, toss to coat well, and let drain. 2. Move slider to AIR FRY/STOVETOP. Select SEAR/SAUTÉ and set to 3. Select START/STOP to begin preheating. Allow unit to preheat for 5 minutes. After 5 minutes, add 1 tablespoon of oil to the pot. Add the onion and sauté until softened, 4 to 5 minutes. Add the minced garlic and roasted garlic and cook until fragrant, 1 minute. 3. Add the courgette, and pepper and cook until softened, 4 to 5 minutes. Add the wine and deglaze the pot, scraping up any browned bits from the bottom and allowing the mixture to reduce by half, about 2 minutes. Carefully transfer the mixture to a big bowl and set aside. 4. Heat the remaining 1 tablespoon of oil in the pot. Add the aubergine and brown, stirring often, 2 to 3 minutes. Press START/STOP to turn off the SEAR/SAUTÉ function. 5. Return the vegetables to the pot, add the stock, basil, and herbes de Provence, and season with salt and pepper. Stir well, then add the tomatoes and their juices. 6. Close the lid and move slider to PRESSURE. Make sure the pressure release valve is in the SEAL position. The temperature will default to HIGH, which is the correct setting. Set time to 6 minutes. Select START/STOP to begin cooking. 7. When cooking is complete, naturally release the pressure for 5 minutes. Then turn the pressure relief valve to the VENT position for quick pressure relief. Move slider to AIR FRY/ STOVETOP to unlock the lid, then carefully open it. 8. Press START/STOP, then select SEAR/SAUTÉ and set the heat to 4. 9. Stir the contents of the pot and let simmer until thickened, about 5 minutes. 10. Sprinkle with chopped basil and grated Parmesan or vegan cheese, serve.

Per Serving: Calories 312; Fat 17.89g; Sodium 1005mg; Carbs 34.67g; Fibre 11.7g; Sugar 19.16g; Protein 9.51g

Delicious Vegetable Shepherd'S Pie

Prep Time: 35 minutes | Cook Time: 55 minutes | Serves: 2

455 g potatoes, peeled and quartered
2 tablespoons butter, divided, plus more for greasing
2 teaspoons oil
1 small onion, diced
2 garlic cloves, minced
160 g dried brown or green lentils, rinsed, sorted, and drained
480 ml vegetable stock
½ tablespoon tomato paste

1 teaspoon fresh thyme or ½ teaspoon dried thyme
Salt
Freshly ground black pepper
100 g shredded Cheddar cheese
60 ml whole milk
1 tablespoon cornflour
2 tablespoons cold water
150 g frozen mixed vegetables

1. Add 240 ml of water to the pressure cooker pot. Place the bottom layer of the Deluxe Reversible Rack in the lower position in the pot and put the potatoes in it. 2. Close the lid and cook on high pressure for 5 minutes. Afterwards, quick release the pressure in the pot and open the lid. 3. Remove the potatoes and the rack from the pot and set aside. Carefully drain the water from the pot, wipe dry, and return to the pressure cooker. 4. Coat a medium casserole dish that fits the pot with butter and set aside. 5. Move slider to AIR FRY/STOVETOP. Select SEAR/SAUTÉ and set to Lo1. Select START/STOP to begin cooking. Heat oil in the pot. Add the onion and sauté until softened, 3 minutes. Add the garlic and sauté for 1 minute. Press START/STOP. 6. Stir in the lentils, tomato paste, stock, and thyme and season with salt and pepper. Close the lid and cook on high pressure for 15 minutes. 7. Meanwhile, transfer the potatoes to a medium bowl and mash with a potato masher. Stir in the cheese, milk, and the 2 tablespoons of butter and season with salt and pepper. Set aside. 8. When the cooking time is up on the lentil mixture, allow about a 10-minute natural release, then open the vent at the top and remove the lid. Select SEAR/SAUTÉ and set to 4. 9. In a small bowl, combine the cornflour and cold water and whisk to mix well. Add to the pot and bring to a simmer, stirring often, until thickened. Add the frozen mixed vegetables to the lentil mixture. 10. Transfer the filling to the prepared casserole dish. Spread the mashed potatoes evenly over the filling, up to the edge of the dish. Season with salt and pepper. 11. Clean the pot and pour in the water. Then place the bottom layer of the Deluxe Reversible Rack in the lower position in the pot. 12. Put the casserole dish on the rack. 13. Close the lid and move slider to the AIR FRY/ STOVETOP. Preheat the pot by selecting BAKE/ ROAST, setting temperature to 175°C, and setting time to 25 minutes. Select START/STOP to begin cooking. Bake until the potatoes are lightly golden brown.

Per Serving: Calories 767; Fat 38.75g; Sodium 1549mg; Carbs 81.23g; Fibre 13.5g; Sugar 14.39g; Protein 27.27g

Tasty Vegan Sloppy Joes

Prep Time: 10 minutes | Cook Time: 20 minutes | Serves: 2

2 tablespoons oil
½ onion, minced
2 garlic cloves, minced
½ green pepper , seeded and diced
1 carrot, grated
2 teaspoons salt
½ tablespoon chili powder, plus more for seasoning (optional)
½ teaspoon dried oregano
Pinch paprika

2 tablespoons tomato paste
1 can crushed roasted tomatoes with their juices
1 tablespoon apple cider vinegar
1 tablespoon vegan Worcestershire sauce, such as Annie's brand
360 ml vegetable stock or water
180 g dried lentils, sorted and rinsed
1 tablespoon maple syrup (optional)
4 large portobello mushroom caps, roasted

1. Move slider to AIR FRY/STOVETOP. Select SEAR/SAUTÉ and set to Lo1. Select START/STOP to begin cooking. Once the pot is hot, add the oil. Add the onion, pepper , garlic, and carrot and sauté until softened, 3 minutes. Stir in the salt, the oregano, ½ tablespoon of chili powder, and paprika. Add the tomato paste and cook, stirring, for 1 minute. 2. Add the tomatoes and their juices, Worcestershire sauce, the vinegar, stock, and lentils and stir well, scraping up any browned bits from the bottom of the pot. 3. Close the lid and move slider to PRESSURE. Make sure the pressure release valve is in the SEAL position. The temperature will default to HIGH, which is the correct setting. Set time to 13 minutes. Select START/STOP to begin cooking. 4. When cooking is complete, naturally release the pressure for 10 minutes. Then turn the pressure relief valve to the VENT position for quick pressure relief. Move slider to AIR FRY/ STOVETOP to unlock the lid, then carefully open it. 5. Stir the sloppy joe filling, seasoning with more chili powder (if desired) and adding the maple syrup (if using). 6. Divide the filling between two of the portobello caps, then top with the remaining portobello caps and serve.
Per Serving: Calories 293; Fat 15.18g; Sodium 1749mg; Carbs 37.77g; Fibre 5.3g; Sugar 18.43g; Protein 8.26g

Orange Wheat Berry Salad

Prep Time: 10 minutes | Cook Time: 35 minutes | Serves: 6

3 tablespoons olive oil, divided
165 g wheat berries
340 ml water, divided
240 g peeled and shredded carrots
2 apples, peeled, cored, and diced small
60 g raisins

2 tablespoons pure maple syrup
2 teaspoons orange zest
60 ml fresh orange juice
1 tablespoon balsamic vinegar
½ teaspoon salt

1. Move slider to AIR FRY/STOVETOP. Select SEAR/SAUTÉ and set to 3. Select START/STOP to begin cooking. Heat 1 tablespoon oil and add wheat berries. Stir-fry for 4 to 5 minutes until browned and fragrant. Add 480 ml water. 2. Close the lid and cook on low pressure for 30 minutes. When cooking is complete, naturally release the pressure for 10 minutes. Then turn the pressure relief valve to the VENT position for quick pressure relief. Move slider to AIR FRY/ STOVETOP to unlock the lid, then carefully open it. 3. Let cool for 10 minutes and drain any additional liquid. 4. Transfer cooled berries to a medium bowl and add remaining ingredients. Refrigerate covered overnight until ready to serve chilled.
Per Serving: Calories 194; Fat 7.44g; Sodium 224mg; Carbs 31.13g; Fibre 4.4g; Sugar 12.45g; Protein 3.21g

Creamy Turnip and Carrot Purée

Prep Time: 10 minutes | Cook Time: 8 minutes | Serves: 6

2 tablespoons olive oil, divided
3 large turnips, peeled and quartered
4 large carrots, peeled and cut into 6 cm pieces
480 ml vegetable stock

1 teaspoon salt
½ teaspoon ground nutmeg
2 tablespoons sour cream

1. Move slider to AIR FRY/STOVETOP. Select SEAR/SAUTÉ and set to 3. Select START/STOP to begin cooking. Heat 1 tablespoon olive oil. Toss turnips and carrots in oil for 1 minute. Add stock. 2. Close the lid and move slider to PRESSURE. Make sure the pressure release valve is in the SEAL position. The temperature will default to HIGH, which is the correct setting. Set time to 8 minutes. Select START/STOP to begin cooking. 3. When cooking is complete, turn the pressure relief valve to the VENT position for quick pressure relief. Move slider to the right to unlock the lid, then carefully open it. 4. Drain vegetables and reserve liquid; set liquid aside. Add 2 tablespoons of reserved liquid plus remaining ingredients to vegetables in the pot. 5. Use an immersion blender to blend until desired smoothness. If too thick, add more liquid 1 tablespoon at a time. Serve warm.

Per Serving: Calories 121; Fat 5.88g; Sodium 674mg; Carbs 15.72g; Fibre 4g; Sugar 6.93g; Protein 2.84g

Garlicky Kale and Potatoes

Prep Time: 10 minutes | Cook Time: 10 minutes | Serves: 4

1 tablespoon olive oil
1 small onion, peeled and diced
1 stalk celery, diced
2 cloves garlic, minced
4 medium potatoes, peeled and diced
2 bunches kale, washed, deveined, and chopped

360 ml vegetable stock
2 teaspoons salt
½ teaspoon ground black pepper
¼ teaspoon caraway seeds
1 tablespoon apple cider vinegar
4 tablespoons sour cream

1. Move slider to AIR FRY/STOVETOP. Select SEAR/SAUTÉ and set to Lo1. Select START/STOP to begin preheating. Allow unit to preheat for 5 minutes. After 5 minutes, heat oil. Add onion and celery and stir-fry 3 to 5 minutes until onions are translucent. Add garlic and cook for an additional minute. 2. Add potatoes in an even layer. Add chopped kale in an even layer. Add stock. 3. Close the lid and move slider to PRESSURE. Make sure the pressure release valve is in the SEAL position. The temperature will default to HIGH, which is the correct setting. Set time to 5 minutes. Select START/STOP to begin cooking. 4. When cooking is complete, naturally release the pressure for 10 minutes. Then turn the pressure relief valve to the VENT position for quick pressure relief. Move slider to AIR FRY/ STOVETOP to unlock the lid, then carefully open it. Then drain stock. 5. Stir in salt, pepper, caraway seeds, and vinegar; slightly mash the potatoes in the pot. Garnish each serving with 1 tablespoon sour cream.

Per Serving: Calories 364; Fat 5.35g; Sodium 1419mg; Carbs 72.26g; Fibre 9.9g; Sugar 5.53g; Protein 9.76g

Quinoa Endive Boats with Pecans

Prep Time: 10 minutes | Cook Time: 3 minutes | Serves: 4

1 tablespoon walnut oil
160 g quinoa
600 ml water
205 g chopped jarred artichoke hearts
300 g diced tomatoes, seeded

½ small red onion, peeled and thinly sliced
2 tablespoons olive oil
1 tablespoon balsamic vinegar
2 heads chicory
120 g roasted pecans

1. Move slider to AIR FRY/STOVETOP. Select SEAR/SAUTÉ and set to Lo1. Select START/STOP to begin cooking. Heat walnut oil. Add quinoa and toss for 1 minute until slightly browned. Add water. 2. Close the lid and move slider to PRESSURE. Make sure the pressure release valve is in the SEAL position. The temperature will default to HIGH, which is the correct setting. Set time to 2 minutes. Select START/STOP to begin cooking. 3. When timer beeps, let pressure release naturally for 10 minutes. Then turn the pressure relief valve to the VENT position for quick pressure relief. Move slider to AIR FRY/ STOVETOP to unlock the lid, then carefully open it. 4. Drain the liquid and transfer quinoa to a serving bowl. 5. Toss the remaining ingredients except chicory leaves and pecans into quinoa. Refrigerate mixture covered until cooled for 1 hour up to overnight. 6. To prepare boats, separate the chicory leaves. Rinse, drain, and divide them among four plates. Top each with ¼ of the quinoa mixture. 7. Distribute 30 g toasted pecans over the top of each endive boat and serve.

Per Serving: Calories 519; Fat 31.33g; Sodium 143mg; Carbs 52.2g; Fibre 18.7g; Sugar 5.35g; Protein 14.9g

Creamy Butternut Squash Mash

Prep Time: 15 minutes | Cook Time: minutes | Serves: 6

360 ml water
900 g butternut squash, peeled, halved, seeded, and cut into 10 cm pieces
55 g butter

2 tablespoons heavy cream, or whole milk
1 tablespoon packed fresh sage leaves, minced
½ teaspoon table salt
½ teaspoon ground black pepper

1. Pour the water into the pot. Then place the bottom layer of the Deluxe Reversible Rack in the lower position in the pot. Pile the butternut squash pieces onto the rack. 2. Close the lid and move slider to PRESSURE. Make sure the pressure release valve is in the SEAL position. The temperature will default to HIGH, which is the correct setting. Set time to 8 minutes. Select START/STOP to begin cooking. 3. When cooking is complete, turn the pressure relief valve to the VENT position for quick pressure relief. Move slider to the right to unlock the lid, then carefully open it. 4. Pick up the rack with food and take it out of the pot. Drain the liquid in the pot. Return all the butternut squash pieces to the pot. 5. Move slider to AIR FRY/STOVETOP. Select SEAR/SAUTÉ and set to Lo1. Select START/STOP to begin cooking. 6. Use a potato masher to begin mashing the squash. Add the butter, sage, salt, cream, and pepper. Continue to mash the ingredients together until as smooth as you like, about 1 minute. Turn off the SEAR/SAUTÉ function. Serve warm.

Per Serving: Calories 148; Fat9.73 g; Sodium 263mg; Carbs 16.46g; Fibre 2.5g; Sugar 0.34g; Protein 1.5g

Easy Maple Glazed Carrots

Prep Time: 15 minutes | Cook Time: 7 minutes | Serves: 8

◆ ◆ ◆ ◆ ◆ ◆

900 g medium carrots, peeled and cut into 2.5 cm pieces
480 ml water

3 tablespoons butter
2 tablespoons maple syrup
½ teaspoon table salt

◆ ◆ ◆ ◆ ◆ ◆

1. Put the carrots and water in the pot. 2. Close the lid and move slider to PRESSURE. Make sure the pressure release valve is in the SEAL position. The temperature will default to HIGH, which is the correct setting. Set time to 3 minutes. Select START/STOP to begin cooking. 3. When cooking is complete, turn the pressure relief valve to the VENT position for quick pressure relief. Move slider to the right to unlock the lid, then carefully open it. Drain the carrots into a colander set in the sink. 4. Move slider to AIR FRY/STOVETOP. Select SEAR/SAUTÉ and set to 3. Select START/STOP to begin cooking. 5. Melt the butter in the cooker. Stir in the syrup and salt until bubbling. Add the carrots and continue cooking, stirring constantly, until the carrots are glazed, 2 to 3 minutes. 6. Turn off the SEAR/SAUTÉ function and remove the pot from the cooker to stop the cooking. Pour the carrots and any remaining glaze into a serving bowl and cool for a couple of minutes before serving.

Per Serving: Calories 98; Fat 4.59g; Sodium 260mg; Carbs 14.22g; Fibre 3.2g; Sugar 8.4g; Protein 1.1g

Herbed Aubergine, Courgette and Tomatoes

Prep Time: 15 minutes | Cook Time: 7 minutes | Serves: 6

◆ ◆ ◆ ◆ ◆ ◆

One can diced tomatoes with or without chiles
2 medium courgette, diced
1 medium aubergine, stemmed and diced (no need to peel)
1 small yellow onion, chopped
Up to 4 medium garlic cloves, peeled and minced (4 teaspoons)

2 tablespoons olive oil
1 tablespoon fresh lemon juice
1 teaspoon dried oregano
1 teaspoon dried thyme
½ teaspoon table salt
½ teaspoon ground black pepper
1 bay leaf

◆ ◆ ◆ ◆ ◆ ◆

1. Combine all the ingredients in the pot. 2. Close the lid and move slider to PRESSURE. Make sure the pressure release valve is in the SEAL position. The temperature will default to HIGH, which is the correct setting. Set time to 7 minutes. Select START/STOP to begin cooking. 3. When cooking is complete, turn the pressure relief valve to the VENT position for quick pressure relief. Move slider to the right to unlock the lid, then carefully open it. 4. Stir well; fish out and discard the bay leaf. Set the lid askew over the pot and set aside for 5 minutes to blend the flavours before serving in small bowls.

Per Serving: Calories 202; Fat 10.05g; Sodium 354mg; Carbs 12g; Fibre 4.1g; Sugar 6.3g; Protein 16.91g

Spicy and Juicy Red Cabbage

Prep Time: 15 minutes | Cook Time: 14 minutes | Serves: 8

❖ ❖ ❖ ❖ ❖ ❖

240 ml pomegranate juice
120 ml plus 1 tablespoon water
55 g packed light brown sugar
1 canned chipotle chile in adobo sauce, stemmed, seeded (if desired), and minced
1 tablespoon adobo sauce from the can of chipotle

chiles
¼ teaspoon table salt
900 g cored and shredded red cabbage
3 large thyme sprigs
2 teaspoons cornflour

❖ ❖ ❖ ❖ ❖ ❖

1. Stir the juice, 120 ml water, brown sugar, adobo sauce, chipotle chile, and salt in pot until the brown sugar dissolves. Add the cabbage and thyme sprigs. Toss well until evenly and thoroughly coated. 2. Close the lid and move slider to PRESSURE. Make sure the pressure release valve is in the SEAL position. The temperature will default to HIGH, which is the correct setting. Set time to 12 minutes. Select START/STOP to begin cooking. 3. When cooking is complete, turn the pressure relief valve to the VENT position for quick pressure relief. Move slider to the right to unlock the lid, then carefully open it. 4. Move slider to AIR FRY/STOVETOP. Select SEAR/SAUTÉ and set to 3. Select START/STOP to begin cooking. 5. Whisk the remaining 1 tablespoon water and the cornflour in a small bowl until smooth. Stir this slurry into the bubbling cabbage mixture. 6. Continue cooking, stirring constantly, until the liquid in the pot thickens to a sauce, 1 to 2 minutes. Press START/STOP to turn off the SEAR/SAUTÉ function. 7. Pour the cabbage and any sauce into a large serving bowl and cool for a couple of minutes before serving.

Per Serving: Calories 107; Fat 4.11g; Sodium 192mg; Carbs 15.26g; Fibre 2.8g; Sugar 8.97g; Protein 4.21g

Beans & Rice–Stuffed Peppers

Prep Time: 15 minutes | Cook Time: 15 minutes | Serves: 4

❖ ❖ ❖ ❖ ❖ ❖

4 large peppers
400 g cooked white rice
1 medium onion, peeled and diced
3 small Roma tomatoes, diced
60 g marinara sauce
115 g corn kernels (cut from the cob is preferred)
50 g sliced black olives

45 g canned cannellini beans, rinsed and drained
45 g canned black beans, rinsed and drained
1 teaspoon sea salt
1 teaspoon garlic powder
120 ml vegetable stock
2 tablespoons grated Parmesan cheese

❖ ❖ ❖ ❖ ❖ ❖

1. Cut off the pepper tops as close to the tops as possible. Hollow out and discard seeds. Poke a few small holes in the bottom of the peppers to allow drippings to drain. 2. In a medium bowl, combine the remaining ingredients except for stock and Parmesan cheese. Stuff equal amounts of mixture into each of the peppers. 3. Pour the stock into the pot. Then place the bottom layer of the Deluxe Reversible Rack in the lower position in the pot. Set the peppers upright on the rack. 4. Close the lid and cook on low pressure for 15 minutes. When timer beeps, turn the pressure relief valve to the VENT position for quick pressure relief. Move slider to the right to unlock the lid, then carefully open it. 5. Serve immediately and garnish with Parmesan cheese.

Per Serving: Calories 239; Fat 2.2g; Sodium 786mg; Carbs 48.47g; Fibre 5.6g; Sugar 7.77g; Protein 8.67g

Chapter 5 — Soup and Stock Recipes

Creamy Beer Cheese Soup

Prep Time: 15 minutes | Cook Time: 10 minutes | Serves: 6

8 tablespoons salted butter
2 shallots, diced
2 large carrots, peeled and diced
1 red pepper , diced
6 cloves garlic, minced or pressed
65 g plain flour
960 ml chicken stock or garlic stock
300 ml beer (a lager or pale ale works best)
1 teaspoon liquid smoke
240 g heavy cream
400 g aged sharp Cheddar cheese, shredded (since this is the key ingredient in the soup, try to find a quality one versus pre-shredded in a bag)
1 package Boursin spread (any flavour) or 100 g cream cheese, cut into chunky cubes
1 tablespoon dried thyme
1 tablespoon Worcestershire sauce
½ tablespoon Old Bay seasoning
¼ teaspoon nutmeg
1 tablespoon hot sauce (optional)
Hot pretzels, for dipping (usually found in the frozen food section of most markets)
Crumbled blue cheese, for garnish (optional)
Mustard oil, for garnish (optional)

1. Add the butter to the pot. Move slider to AIR FRY/STOVETOP. Select SEAR/SAUTÉ and set to Hi5. Select START/STOP to begin cooking. Once the butter's melted, add the shallots, pepper , carrots, and garlic and sauté for 5 minutes, until slightly softened. 2. Add the flour and quickly stir until the veggies are nice and coated. 3. Add the stock, beer, and liquid smoke and stir to combine well, ensuring any lumps are gone. Scrape the bottom of the pot as well to ensure no flour's caked onto it. Press START/STOP to turn off the SEAR/SAUTÉ function. 4. Close the lid and move slider to PRESSURE. Make sure the pressure release valve is in the SEAL position. The temperature will default to HIGH, which is the correct setting. Set time to 5 minutes. Select START/STOP to begin cooking. 5. When cooking is complete, turn the pressure relief valve to the VENT position for quick pressure relief. Move slider to the right to unlock the lid, then carefully open it. 6. Add the cream to the pot and whisk in with the now-thickened stock. Then, whisk in the Cheddar and Boursin, in batches, until smooth. Follow by whisking in the thyme, Worcestershire, Old Bay, nutmeg, and hot sauce (if using) until fully combined. 7. Puree the soup by using an immersion blender or in batches in a regular blender. 8. Serve with hot pretzels and top with blue cheese crumbles and mustard oil, if desired.

Per Serving: Calories 758; Fat 53.99g; Sodium 1842mg; Carbs 36.24g; Fibre 1.9g; Sugar 5.93g; Protein 32.48g

Lemony Orzo Egg Soup

Prep Time: 15 minutes | Cook Time: 10 minutes | Serves: 6

1.4 L chicken stock
155 g uncooked orzo
For Topping:
Crumbled feta cheese (optional)

3 large eggs
Juice of 2 lemons

1. Place the chicken stock and orzo in the pot. 2. Close the lid and move slider to PRESSURE. Make sure the pressure release valve is in the SEAL position. The temperature will default to HIGH, which is the correct setting. Set time to 5 minutes. Select START/STOP to begin cooking. 3. While the stock and orzo are cooking, whisk the eggs and lemon juice in a bowl and beat with a fork until totally combined. Set aside. 4. When cooking is complete, turn the pressure relief valve to the VENT position for quick pressure relief. Move slider to the right to unlock the lid, then carefully open it. 5. Move slider to AIR FRY/STOVETOP. Select SEAR/SAUTÉ and set to Lo1. Select START/STOP to begin cooking. Stirring all the time, slowly pour 240 ml of the cooked stock into the lemon-egg mixture to temper and stir until totally combined. 6. While still stirring, slowly pour the lemon-egg-stock mixture into the pot, stirring for a good 3 minutes, until the mixture looks creamy and there is no unincorporated egg visible anywhere. Press START/STOP to turn off the SEAR/SAUTÉ function and serve topped with some crumbled feta, if desired.

Per Serving: Calories 164; Fat 8.25g; Sodium 1159mg; Carbs 17.1g; Fibre 1.6g; Sugar 14.12g; Protein 7.28g

Beef, Barley and Red Potato Soup

Prep Time: 15 minutes | Cook Time: 30 minutes | Serves: 6

2 tablespoons extra-virgin olive oil
1 yellow onion, diced
1 large carrot, peeled and diced
2 ribs celery, sliced 1 cm thick
900 g chuck meat, cut into 2.5 cm cubes
6 cloves garlic, minced
1.4 L beef stock

175 g pearl barley, rinsed
1 tablespoon Worcestershire sauce
1½ tablespoons seasoned salt
2 teaspoons dried thyme
1 teaspoon black pepper
455 g baby red potatoes, skins on, quartered
2 bay leaves

1. Add the olive oil to the pot. Move slider to AIR FRY/STOVETOP. Select SEAR/SAUTÉ and set to Hi5. Select START/STOP to begin cooking. After heating for 3 minutes, add the onion, carrot, and celery and sauté for 5 minutes, until softened. 2. Add the beef and garlic and sear the beef on all sides for another 2–3 minutes, until the edges are nicely browned. 3. Add the stock, Worcestershire sauce, barley, seasoned salt, thyme, and black pepper, and use a wooden spoon to scrape up any browned bits from the bottom of the pot, then add the potatoes and bay leaves. Press START/STOP to turn off the SEAR/SAUTÉ function. 4. Close the lid and move slider to PRESSURE. Make sure the pressure release valve is in the SEAL position. The temperature will default to HIGH, which is the correct setting. Set time to 20 minutes. Select START/STOP to begin cooking. 5. When the cook time is complete, naturally release the pressure for 15 minutes. Then turn the pressure relief valve to the VENT position for quick pressure relief. Serve.

Per Serving: Calories 468; Fat 13.89g; Sodium 1835mg; Carbs 44.53g; Fibre 7.7g; Sugar 3.3g; Protein 42.51g

Traditional Vegetable Stock

Prep Time: 10 minutes | Cook Time: 1½ hours | Serves: 8

8 stalks celery, cut in half
4 medium sweet onions, peeled and quartered
4 medium carrots, cut in half
4 Roma tomatoes, cut in half
1 fennel bulb, quartered
1 medium green pepper , seeded and quartered

4 cloves garlic, peeled and crushed
2 tablespoons olive oil
5 sprigs fresh parsley
5 sprigs fresh tarragon
2 bay leaves

1. Place celery, carrots, onions, tomatoes, pepper , fennel, and garlic on a large rimmed baking sheet. Drizzle with oil and toss to coat. 2. Place the bottom layer of the Deluxe Reversible Rack in the lower position in the pot. Place the baking sheet on the rack. 3. Close the lid and move slider to the AIR FRY/ STOVETOP. Preheat the pot by selecting BAKE/ ROAST, setting temperature to 200°C, and setting time to 1 hour. Select START/STOP to begin cooking. 4. Turning vegetables every 10 minutes to avoid burning. If vegetables start to blacken, remove them from the baking sheet. 5. Once done, remove the baking sheet and rack. Add the roasted vegetables, parsley, tarragon, and bay leaves to the pot, then poor in the water to cover the vegetables. 6. Close the lid and cook on low pressure for 30 minutes. 7. When cooking is complete, naturally release the pressure for 30 minutes. Then turn the pressure relief valve to the VENT position for quick pressure relief. Move slider to AIR FRY/ STOVETOP to unlock the lid, then carefully open it. 8. Strain stock into a jar and use immediately, refrigerate for up to seven days, or freeze for up to three months.

Per Serving: Calories 127; Fat 3.91g; Sodium 68mg; Carbs 22.19g; Fibre 4.5g; Sugar 13.06g; Protein 3.12g

Butternut Squash Soup

Prep Time: 15 minutes | Cook Time: 25 minutes | Serves: 6

1 tablespoon olive oil
1 small onion, peeled and diced
2 celery stalks, sliced
1.3 kg butternut squash, peeled, seeded, and cubed
1 small Granny Smith apple, peeled, cored, and diced
1 teaspoon sea salt

¼ teaspoon white pepper
1 teaspoon celery seed
¼ teaspoon ground nutmeg
¼ teaspoon hot sauce
2.5 cm piece of fresh ginger, peeled and minced
960 ml chicken stock

1. Move slider to AIR FRY/STOVETOP. Select SEAR/SAUTÉ and set to 3. Select START/STOP to begin cooking. Heat the oil. Add the onion and celery. Sauté for 5 minutes until onions are translucent. Add the butternut squash and apple. Continue to sauté for 2–3 minutes until apples are tender. Add remaining ingredients. 2. Close the lid and move slider to PRESSURE. Make sure the pressure release valve is in the SEAL position. The temperature will default to HIGH, which is the correct setting. Set time to 15 minutes. Select START/STOP to begin cooking. 3. When cooking is complete, turn the pressure relief valve to the VENT position for quick pressure relief. Move slider to the right to unlock the lid, then carefully open it. 4. In the pot, purée soup with an immersion blender. Ladle into bowls and serve warm.

Per Serving: Calories 385; Fat 13.74g; Sodium 1064mg; Carbs 29.71g; Fibre 4.5g; Sugar 2.89g; Protein 36.75g

Lime Chicken Tortilla Soup

Prep Time: 15 minutes | Cook Time: 20 minutes | Serves: 6

2 tablespoons vegetable oil
1 yellow onion, diced
2 jalapeño peppers, diced
3 cloves garlic, minced or pressed
1.2 L chicken stock
1 can diced tomatoes, with their juices (any variety will do)

To Serve:

Chopped fresh coriander
Freshly sliced avocado

Juice of 2 limes
2 tablespoons hot sauce
2 tablespoons salsa verde
1 tablespoon dried coriander
1 tablespoon ground cumin
900 g boneless, skinless chicken breasts or thighs
120 g sour cream

Shredded Mexican cheese
Tortilla strips

1. Pour the vegetable oil into the pot. Move slider to AIR FRY/STOVETOP. Select SEAR/SAUTÉ and set to Hi5. Select START/STOP to begin cooking. when the oil is heated, add the onion and jalapeños and cook for 3 to 5 minutes, until softened. Add the garlic and sauté for 1 minute longer. 2. Add the chicken stock, diced tomatoes, hot sauce, salsa verde, dried coriander, lime juice, and cumin. Stir well. Press START/STOP to turn off the SEAR/SAUTÉ function. 3. Add the chicken breasts. Close the lid and move slider to PRESSURE. Make sure the pressure release valve is in the SEAL position. The temperature will default to HIGH, which is the correct setting. Set time to 14 minutes. Select START/STOP to begin cooking. 4. Quick release when done and let the soup cool for about 5 minutes. 5. In the meantime, use tongs to remove the chicken. Place in a mixing bowl and shred with two forks (or a hand/stand mixer for ease) and set aside. 6. Once the soup has slightly cooled, whisk in the sour cream until totally melded. Return the shredded chicken to the pot and stir. 7. Serve topped with some fresh coriander, avocado, shredded cheese, and tortilla strips.

Per Serving: Calories 523; Fat 26.79g; Sodium 1483mg; Carbs 46.69g; Fibre 7g; Sugar 13.9g; Protein 23.3g

Tangy Pork Stock

Prep Time: 5 minutes | Cook Time: 1½ hours | Serves: 8

1.8 kg cooked pork bones
2 stalks celery, chopped
1 medium white onion, peeled and quartered
1 medium carrot, peeled and chopped

2 cloves garlic, peeled and crushed
2 sprigs fresh thyme
1 sprig fresh sage

1. Place all ingredients in the pot, then then poor in the water to cover the ingredients. 2. Close the lid and cook on low pressure for 90 minutes. 3. When cooking is complete, naturally release the pressure for 30 minutes. Then turn the pressure relief valve to the VENT position for quick pressure relief. Move slider to AIR FRY/ STOVETOP to unlock the lid, then carefully open it. 4. Strain stock into a jar and use immediately, refrigerate for up to seven days, or freeze for up to three months.

Per Serving: Calories 486; Fat 25.17g; Sodium 134mg; Carbs 2.69g; Fibre 0.7g; Sugar 1.01g; Protein 58.44g

Savoury Lentil Soup

3 tablespoons extra-virgin olive oil
1 medium yellow onion, diced
2 medium carrots, peeled and diced
2 ribs celery, thinly sliced
3 cloves garlic, minced or pressed
1.4 L vegetable stock
2 teaspoons seasoned salt
2 teaspoons dried thyme

1½ teaspoons cumin
1 teaspoon black pepper
1 teaspoon dried basil
1½ teaspoons curry powder (optional, for spice)
265 g brown or green lentils, rinsed in cold water and drained
125 – 200 g baby spinach (optional)

1. Pour the oil into the pot. Move slider to AIR FRY/STOVETOP. Select SEAR/SAUTÉ and set to Hi5. Select START/STOP to begin cooking. Heat the oil for 3 minutes, then add the onion, carrots, and celery and sauté for 5 minutes, until slightly softened. Add the garlic and sauté for 1 minute longer. 2. Pour in the vegetable stock and use a wooden spoon to scrape up any browned bits from the bottom of the pot. Stir in the seasoned salt, thyme, cumin, black pepper, basil, and curry powder (if using). Then, add the rinsed lentils. Rest the spinach on top but do not stir. Press START/STOP to turn off the SEAR/SAUTÉ function. 3. Close the lid and move slider to PRESSURE. Make sure the pressure release valve is in the SEAL position. The temperature will default to HIGH, which is the correct setting. Set time to 15 minutes. Select START/STOP to begin cooking. 4. When done, allow a 5-minute natural release followed by a quick release. 5. Stir everything up and serve.

Per Serving: Calories 155; Fat 5.62g; Sodium 1448mg; Carbs 22.61g; Fibre 5.7g; Sugar 5.85g; Protein 6.23g

Savoury Ham Stock

1 cooked ham bone
2 stalks celery, chopped
1 medium yellow onion, peeled and quartered
1 medium carrot, peeled and chopped

2 cloves garlic, peeled and crushed
5 sprigs fresh coriander
2 bay leaves

1. Place all ingredients in the pot, then then poor in the water to cover the ingredients. 2. Close the lid and cook on low pressure for one hour. When cooking is complete, turn the pressure relief valve to the VENT position for quick pressure relief. Move slider to the right to unlock the lid, then carefully open it. 3. Strain stock into a jar and use immediately, refrigerate for up to seven days, or freeze for up to three months.

Per Serving: Calories 127; Fat 3.92g; Sodium 1460mg; Carbs 3.65g; Fibre 0.6g; Sugar 1.02g; Protein 19.5g

Beef and Rice Soup

Prep Time: 15 minutes | Cook Time: 40 minutes | Serves: 6

2 tablespoons butter
1 medium yellow onion, chopped
675 g beef bottom round, cut into 2.5 cm pieces
2 medium garlic cloves, peeled and minced (2 teaspoons)
1.4 L beef or chicken stock
70 g raw long-grain brown rice

1 medium turnip, peeled and diced
2 medium carrots, thinly sliced
2 teaspoons dried oregano
2 teaspoons dried thyme
¼ teaspoon table salt
Ground black pepper for garnishing

1. Move slider to AIR FRY/STOVETOP. Select SEAR/SAUTÉ and set to 3. Select START/STOP to begin preheating. Allow unit to preheat for 2 minutes. After 2 minutes, melt the butter in the pot. Add the onion and cook, stirring frequently, until softened, about 4 minutes. 2. Add the beef and garlic; continue cooking, stirring once in a while, until all the pieces of beef have lost their raw, red colour, about 4 minutes. 3. Pour in the stock and scrape up every speck of browned stuff on the pot's bottom. Press START/STOP to turn off the SEAR/SAUTÉ function. Stir in the rice. 4. Close the lid and move slider to PRESSURE. Make sure the pressure release valve is in the SEAL position. The temperature will default to HIGH, which is the correct setting. Set time to 30 minutes. Select START/STOP to begin cooking. 5. When cooking is complete, turn the pressure relief valve to the VENT position for quick pressure relief. Move slider to the right to unlock the lid, then carefully open it. 6. Stir in the turnip, carrots, oregano, thyme, and salt. Close the lid and still cook on high pressure for 6 minutes. 7. When the timer beeps, allow a 30-minute natural release followed by a quick release. Open the lid and stir well before serving. 8. Garnish the bowls with lots of ground black pepper.

Per Serving: Calories 259; Fat 8.77g; Sodium 426mg; Carbs 16.82g; Fibre 2.5g; Sugar 4.44g; Protein 27.51g

Beef, Rice, and Green Lentil Soup

Prep Time: 15 minutes | Cook Time: 1 hour and 25 minutes | Serves: 6

2 tablespoons butter
1 large beef shank
3 medium carrots, thinly sliced
3 medium celery stalks, thinly sliced
1 medium yellow onion, chopped
1.4 L beef or chicken stock

1 teaspoon dried thyme
1 teaspoon ground coriander
½ teaspoon ground cinnamon
¼ teaspoon table salt
100 g raw long-grain brown rice
90 g green lentils

1. Move slider to AIR FRY/STOVETOP. Select SEAR/SAUTÉ and set to 3. Select START/STOP to begin preheating. Allow unit to preheat for 2 minutes. After 2 minutes, melt the butter in the pot. 2. Add the beef shank and brown well on both sides, turning a couple of times, about 8 minutes. Transfer to a nearby bowl. 3. Add the carrots, onion and celery to the pot. Cook, stirring often, until the onion begins to soften, about 4 minutes. Pour in the stock, turn off the SEAR/SAUTÉ function, and scrape up the browned bits on the pot's bottom. Stir in the thyme, coriander, cinnamon, and salt. Return the shank and any juices in the bowl to the pot. 4. Close the lid and move slider to PRESSURE. Make sure the pressure release valve is in the SEAL position. The temperature will default to HIGH, which is the correct setting. Set time to 45 minutes. Select START/STOP to begin cooking. 5. When cooking is complete, turn the pressure relief valve to the VENT position for quick pressure relief. Move slider to the right to unlock the lid, then carefully open it. Stir in the rice and lentils. 6. Close the lid and still cook on high pressure for 30 minutes. 7. Again, use the quick-release method to bring the pot's pressure back to normal. Open the lid and transfer the shank to a cutting board. Remove the meat from the bone and discard the bone; chop the meat into spoon-sized bits. 8. Stir these back into the soup before serving.

Per Serving: Calories 539; Fat 42.61g; Sodium 1122mg; Carbs 16.74g; Fibre 1.3g; Sugar 2.17g; Protein 21.61g

Cheese Sausage Beer Soup

Prep Time: 15 minutes | Cook Time: 20 minutes | Serves: 6

1 to 2 tablespoons butter
900 g smoked kielbasa, cut into 2.5 cm sections
1 medium yellow onion, chopped
1 teaspoon dried sage
1 teaspoon dried thyme
½ teaspoon grated nutmeg

¼ teaspoon table salt
1 L chicken stock
300 ml bottle golden beer, preferably a pilsner
120 ml whole milk
2 tablespoons plain flour
150 g sharp American Cheddar cheese, shredded

1. Move slider to AIR FRY/STOVETOP. Select SEAR/SAUTÉ and set to 3. Select START/STOP to begin preheating. Allow unit to preheat for 2 minutes. After 2 minutes, melt the butter in the pot. 2. Add the sausage pieces and cook, stirring occasionally, until lightly browned, about 4 minutes. Add the onion and continue cooking, stirring more often, until the onion begins to soften, about 3 minutes. 3. Stir in the sage, nutmeg, thyme, and salt until fragrant, just a few seconds. Pour in the stock and scrape up the browned bits on the pot's bottom. Press START/STOP to turn off the SEAR/SAUTÉ function and pour in the beer. Stir a few times to reduce the foam, then close the lid. 4. Close the lid and move slider to PRESSURE. Make sure the pressure release valve is in the SEAL position. The temperature will default to HIGH, which is the correct setting. Set time to 7 minutes. Select START/STOP to begin cooking. 5. When cooking is complete, turn the pressure relief valve to the VENT position for quick pressure relief. Move slider to the right to unlock the lid, then carefully open it. 6. Move slider to AIR FRY/STOVETOP. Select SEAR/SAUTÉ and set to 3. Select START/STOP to begin cooking. 7. Bring the soup to a simmer, stirring occasionally. Whisk the milk and flour in a small bowl until smooth and uniform. 8. Whisk this slurry into the simmering soup and continue cooking, whisking constantly, until slightly thickened, 1 to 2 minutes. Turn off the SEAR/SAUTÉ function and stir in the cheese. Let rest for 5 minutes to melt the cheese and blend the flavours.

Per Serving: Calories 497; Fat 32.51g; Sodium 1878mg; Carbs 22.93g; Fibre 1.8g; Sugar 9.6g; Protein 28.04g

Lamb and Potato Soup

✧ ✧ ✧ ✧ ✧

2 medium garlic cloves, peeled and minced (2 teaspoons)
1 teaspoon dried thyme
1 teaspoon dried oregano
½ teaspoon ground dried turmeric
¼ teaspoon grated nutmeg
½ teaspoon table salt
2 tablespoons olive oil
455 g boneless leg of lamb, any large pieces of fat removed, the meat cut into 2.5 cm pieces
1 medium red onion, chopped
2 L chicken stock
455 g medium parsnips, peeled and cut into 2.5 cm pieces
455 g small yellow potatoes such as Yukon Golds, none larger than a golf ball, each quartered
10 g loosely packed fresh coriander leaves, finely chopped

✧ ✧ ✧ ✧ ✧

1. In a large bowl, mix together the lamb, garlic, thyme, turmeric, oregano, nutmeg, and salt until the meat is evenly coated. Set aside for 10 minutes. 2. Move slider to AIR FRY/STOVETOP. Select SEAR/SAUTÉ and set to 3. Select START/STOP to begin preheating. Allow unit to preheat for 2 minutes. After 2 minutes, warm the oil in the pot for one minute. Add the onion and cook, stirring frequently, until it just begins to soften, about 4 minutes. Add the lamb and every speck of its rub. Cook, stirring often, until the lamb loses its raw, pink colour, about 3 minutes. 3. Pour in the stock, press START/STOP to turn off the SEAR/SAUTÉ function, and scrape up any browned bits on the pot's bottom. 4. Close the lid and move slider to PRESSURE. Make sure the pressure release valve is in the SEAL position. The temperature will default to HIGH, which is the correct setting. Set time to 15 minutes. Select START/STOP to begin cooking. 5. When cooking is complete, turn the pressure relief valve to the VENT position for quick pressure relief. Move slider to the right to unlock the lid, then carefully open it. Stir in the parsnips and potatoes. Lock the lid back onto the pot. Still cook on high pressure for 7 minutes. 6. Again, use the quick-release method to bring the pot's pressure back to normal. Open the lid and stir in the coriander, then set the lid askew over the pot for 5 minutes to blend the flavours. Stir well before serving.

Per Serving: Calories 281; Fat 9.89g; Sodium 1496mg; Carbs 30.44g; Fibre 3.9g; Sugar 17.57g; Protein 19.48g

Prawn and Rice Soup

Prep Time: 10 minutes | Cook Time: 12 minutes | Serves: 6

1 L chicken stock
One can crushed tomatoes
1 medium yellow onion, chopped
240 ml regular or low-fat coconut milk
1 medium green pepper , stemmed, cored, and chopped
2 medium celery stalks, thinly sliced
100 g raw long-grain white rice, preferably jasmine or basmati
Up to 2 small jalapeño chiles, stemmed, seeded, and finely chopped
2 tablespoons packed fresh oregano leaves, minced
675 g medium prawn, peeled and deveined
10 g loosely packed fresh parsley leaves, chopped
2 teaspoons fresh lemon juice

1. Add the stock, tomatoes, coconut milk, onion, pepper , celery, rice, chiles, and oregano to the pot, stir to mix well. 2. Close the lid and move slider to PRESSURE. Make sure the pressure release valve is in the SEAL position. The temperature will default to HIGH, which is the correct setting. Set time to 10 minutes. Select START/STOP to begin cooking. 3. When cooking is complete, turn the pressure relief valve to the VENT position for quick pressure relief. Move slider to the right to unlock the lid, then carefully open it. 4. Move slider to AIR FRY/STOVETOP. Select SEAR/SAUTÉ and set to Lo1. Select START/STOP to begin cooking. 5. Stir the prawn, parsley, and lemon juice into the soup. Continue cooking, stirring often, until the prawn are pink and firm, about 2 minutes. Turn off the SEAR/SAUTÉ function and serve warm.

Per Serving: Calories 342; Fat 8.9g; Sodium 1377mg; Carbs 30.64g; Fibre 2.6g; Sugar 5.53g; Protein 34.11g

Prawn Stock

Prep Time: 5 minutes | Cook Time: 30 minutes | Serves: 8

455 g prawn shells and heads
1 medium yellow onion, peeled and chopped
2 stalks celery, chopped
1 large carrot, peeled and chopped
3 cloves garlic, peeled and smashed
2 bay leaves
1 teaspoon seafood seasoning
½ teaspoon salt

1. Place all ingredients in the pot, then then poor in the water to cover the ingredients. 2. Close the lid and move slider to PRESSURE. Make sure the pressure release valve is in the SEAL position. The temperature will default to HIGH, which is the correct setting. Set time to 30 minutes. Select START/STOP to begin cooking. 3. When the timer beeps, let pressure release naturally, about 30 minutes. Open the lid. 4. Strain stock into a jar and use immediately, refrigerate for up to three days, or freeze for up to three months.

Per Serving: Calories 70; Fat 0.83g; Sodium 675mg; Carbs 2.97g; Fibre 0.7g; Sugar 1.12g; Protein 11.94g

Fish & Butternut Squash Soup

Prep Time: 15 minutes | Cook Time: 15 minutes | Serves: 6

1.4 L chicken stock

1 medium leek white and pale green parts only, halved lengthwise, washed well, and thinly sliced

1 very small butternut squash, diced, peeled, and seeded

Up to 2 fresh medium jalapeño chiles, stemmed and thinly sliced

2 medium garlic cloves, peeled and slivered

10 g loosely packed coriander leaves, chopped

½ teaspoon ground allspice

½ teaspoon ground cinnamon

½ teaspoon table salt

900 g skinned sea bass, cut into 2.5 cm pieces

1. Combine the stock, butternut squash, leek, garlic, coriander, chilies, allspice, cinnamon, and salt in the pot. 2. Close the lid and move slider to PRESSURE. Make sure the pressure release valve is in the SEAL position. The temperature will default to HIGH, which is the correct setting. Set time to 7 minutes. Select START/STOP to begin cooking. 3. When cooking is complete, turn the pressure relief valve to the VENT position for quick pressure relief. Move slider to the right to unlock the lid, then carefully open it. Stir well. 4. Move slider to AIR FRY/STOVETOP. Select SEAR/SAUTÉ and set to 3. Select START/STOP to begin cooking. 5. Bring the soup to a simmer. Add the fish and cook, stirring occasionally but gently, until cooked through, 4 to 5 minutes. Press START/STOP to turn off the SEAR/SAUTÉ function and remove the hot pot to keep the fish from overcooking.

Per Serving: Calories 255; Fat 8.19g; Sodium 1204mg; Carbs 9.54g; Fibre 1.5g; Sugar 2.83g; Protein 36.96g

Simple Fish Stock

Prep Time: 5 minutes | Cook Time: 30 minutes | Serves: 8

455 g fish bones and heads

1 medium yellow onion, peeled and chopped

2 stalks celery, chopped

1 large carrot, peeled and chopped

3 cloves garlic, peeled and smashed

1 bay leaf

10 whole black peppercorns

½ teaspoon salt

60 ml white wine

1. Place all ingredients in the pot, then then poor in the water to cover the ingredients. 2. Close the lid and move slider to PRESSURE. Make sure the pressure release valve is in the SEAL position. The temperature will default to HIGH, which is the correct setting. Set time to 30 minutes. Select START/STOP to begin cooking. 3. When cooking is complete, naturally release the pressure for 30 minutes. Then turn the pressure relief valve to the VENT position for quick pressure relief. Move slider to AIR FRY/ STOVETOP to unlock the lid, then carefully open it. 4. Strain stock into a jar and use immediately, refrigerate for up to three days, or freeze for up to three months.

Per Serving: Calories 131; Fat 6.56g; Sodium 330mg; Carbs 3.01g; Fibre 0.7g; Sugar 1.16g; Protein 14.37g

Creamy Herbed Chicken with Mushroom

Prep Time: 15 minutes | Cook Time: 23 minutes | Serves: 3

2 tbsp (28 g) grass-fed butter or ghee
1 medium yellow onion, thinly sliced
680 g mushrooms, cut into thirds, woody ends removed
5 cloves garlic, chopped
120 ml dry white wine
2 large celery ribs with leaves, thinly sliced
1 tsp sea salt
15 g finely chopped fresh flat-leaf parsley, plus more

for garnish
1 tbsp (2 g) finely chopped fresh rosemary
1 tbsp (4 g) finely chopped fresh dill
2 tsp (2 g) finely chopped fresh thyme leaves
2 boneless, skinless chicken breasts
175 ml chicken or vegetable stock
175 ml heavy cream
2 tbsp (15 g) gluten-free plain flour
20 g shredded Parmesan cheese, plus more for garnish

1. Add butter to the pot. Move slider to AIR FRY/STOVETOP. Select SEAR/SAUTÉ and set to 3. Select START/STOP to begin cooking. Once the fat butter melted, add the onion and mushrooms and sauté, stirring occasionally, for 7 minutes, or until caramelised. 2. Then, add the garlic and sauté for 1 minute, stirring occasionally. Add the wine and deglaze the pot, scraping up any browned bits with a wooden spoon. Press START/STOP to turn off the SEAR/SAUTÉ function. 3. Add the celery, salt, parsley, dill, thyme, rosemary, chicken and stock, ensuring the chicken is submerged in the liquid. 4. Close the lid and move slider to PRESSURE. Make sure the pressure release valve is in the SEAL position. The temperature will default to HIGH, which is the correct setting. Set time to 9 minutes. Select START/STOP to begin cooking. 5. Meanwhile, place the cream in a big measuring cup or medium bowl, then sprinkle the flour on the top, whisking until the flour is mostly incorporated. Set aside. 6. Once the timer beeps, turn the pressure relief valve to the VENT position for quick pressure relief. Move slider to the right to unlock the lid, then carefully open it. 7. With tongs, transfer the chicken to a plate or cutting board. Chop the chicken into bite-size chunks, then set aside. 8. Move slider to AIR FRY/STOVETOP. Select SEAR/SAUTÉ and set to 3. Select START/STOP to begin cooking. Add the cream mixture and the Parmesan to the pot, allowing the mixture to come to a simmer, then quickly stir until the cream and Parmesan are fully mixed in. Simmer for about 5 minutes, or until the liquid slightly thickens. Press START/STOP. 9. Add the chicken and stir well. Taste for seasoning and adjust the salt to taste. Allow it to rest for 10 minutes. 10. Serve immediately, garnished with shredded Parmesan and chopped fresh parsley.

Per Serving: Calories 1234; Fat 35.35g; Sodium 1642mg; Carbs 185.63g; Fibre 28.2g; Sugar 7.19g; Protein 72.32g

Peanut Butter Chicken

Prep Time: 15 minutes | Cook Time: 8 minutes | Serves: 6

130 g smooth peanut butter
60 ml soy sauce or gluten-free tamari
60 ml honey
60 ml rice vinegar
160 ml chicken stock
3 cloves garlic, minced
905 g chicken breast

80 ml full-fat canned coconut milk
558 to 744 g cooked rice or 330 to 440 g cauliflower rice, for serving
3 tbsp (8 g) chopped fresh coriander (optional)
3 tbsp (27 g) chopped peanuts (optional)
Salt
Freshly ground black pepper

1. Mix together the peanut butter, honey, vinegar, soy sauce, chicken stock and garlic in a bowl. 2. Place the chicken in the pot. Pour the peanut butter sauce on top. 3. Close the lid and move slider to PRESSURE. Make sure the pressure release valve is in the SEAL position. The temperature will default to HIGH, which is the correct setting. Set time to 8 minutes. Select START/STOP to begin cooking. 4. When cooking is complete, turn the pressure relief valve to the VENT position for quick pressure relief. Move slider to the right to unlock the lid, then carefully open it. 5. Pour in the coconut milk. You can cut or shred the chicken into smaller pieces, or keep as a larger breast. 6. Serve warm over rice or cauliflower rice. Garnish with fresh coriander and peanuts (if using). Sprinkle with salt and pepper to taste.

Per Serving: Calories 562; Fat 30.91g; Sodium 1166mg; Carbs 29.99g; Fibre 4.3g; Sugar 17.19g; Protein 43.75g

Lemony Chicken with Artichoke

Prep Time: 15 minutes | Cook Time: 10 minutes | Serves: 4

½ tsp sea salt, plus more to taste
½ tsp freshly ground black pepper
680 g boneless, skinless chicken breast or thighs
237 ml dry white wine, e. g. , chardonnay; or chicken stock
Juice of 1 large lemon (about 60 ml)
2 tsp (4 g) garam masala
1 tsp ground turmeric
1 clove garlic, crushed

1 (170 g) can hearts of palm, drained
1 (170 g) jar artichoke hearts, drained
3 sprigs thyme
1 lemon, sliced
2 tsp (4 g) lemon pepper
3 tbsp (24 g) cornflour
2 tbsp (30 ml) water
Cooked rice, cauliflower rice, pasta or cooked vegetables, for serving

1. Season the chicken with salt and pepper. Place in the pot. 2. In a small bowl, mix together the wine, garam masala, lemon juice, turmeric and garlic. Pour on top of the chicken. 3. Cover the chicken with the hearts of palm, artichoke hearts, thyme and lemon slices and sprinkle with the lemon pepper. 4. Close the lid and move slider to PRESSURE. Make sure the pressure release valve is in the SEAL position. The temperature will default to HIGH, which is the correct setting. Set time to 9 minutes. Select START/STOP to begin cooking. 5. When cooking is complete, turn the pressure relief valve to the VENT position for quick pressure relief. Move slider to the right to unlock the lid, then carefully open it. 6. In a small bowl, whisk together the cornflour and the water and add to the sauce. Continue to stir until thickened. Remove the thyme sprigs. 7. Serve the chicken on top of rice, cauliflower rice or pasta, or with vegetables.

Per Serving: Calories 407; Fat 10.18g; Sodium 780mg; Carbs 61.26g; Fibre 6.9g; Sugar 18.92g; Protein 18.7g

Cheese Beef and Quinoa Bowls

Prep Time: 15 minutes | Cook Time: 12 minutes | Serves: 6

* * * * * *

4 slices raw bacon, diced
1 yellow onion, diced
455 g 90% lean minced beef
½ tsp ground mustard powder
½ tsp onion powder
1 tsp salt
½ tsp freshly ground black pepper
1 (410 g) can fire-roasted diced tomatoes
173 g uncooked quinoa

240 ml water
1 tbsp (14 g) mayonnaise
1 tbsp (16 g) barbecue sauce
1 tbsp (11 g) prepared yellow mustard
2 tbsp (30 g) ketchup
115 g shredded cheddar cheese
75 g diced kosher dill pickles
90 g diced Roma tomatoes

* * * * * *

1. Move slider to AIR FRY/STOVETOP. Select SEAR/SAUTÉ and set to 3. Select START/STOP to begin preheating. Allow unit to preheat for 2 minutes. After 2 minutes, add the bacon and cook until crisp. Remove and transfer to a paper towel-lined plate. 2. Add the onion, beef, onion powder, mustard powder, salt and pepper. Break apart the beef using a wooden spoon. Once the onion begins to turn translucent, about 3 minutes, press START/STOP. 3. Stir in the can of tomatoes, quinoa and water. 4. Close the lid and move slider to PRESSURE. Make sure the pressure release valve is in the SEAL position. The temperature will default to HIGH, which is the correct setting. Set time to 1 minute. Select START/STOP to begin cooking. 5. When cooking is complete, naturally release the pressure for 10 minutes. Then turn the pressure relief valve to the VENT position for quick pressure relief. Move slider to AIR FRY/ STOVETOP to unlock the lid, then carefully open it. 6. Move slider to AIR FRY/STOVETOP. Select SEAR/SAUTÉ and set to 4. Select START/STOP to begin. Stir in the barbecue sauce, mayonnaise, mustard and ketchup. Sauté for 2 minutes while stirring. 7. Press START/STOP. Transfer the quinoa to a serving bowl and top with the cheese, pickles and tomatoes.

Per Serving: Calories 457; Fat 24.47g; Sodium 954mg; Carbs 26.76g; Fibre 4.2g; Sugar 5.49g; Protein 32.16g

Pulled Turkey in Cranberry–Sweet Potato Sauce

Prep Time: 15 minutes | Cook Time: 25 minutes | Serves: 8

* * * * * *

180 ml chicken stock
120 g whole berry cranberry sauce
2 tablespoons packed fresh sage leaves, finely chopped
2 teaspoons fresh thyme leaves

1 teaspoon table salt
1 small sweet potato (about 200 g), peeled and shredded through the large holes of a box grater
1.2 kg boneless skinless turkey tenderloins

* * * * * *

1. Mix the stock, cranberry sauce, thyme, sage, and salt in the pot. Stir in the shredded sweet potato, then place the turkey into this sauce, toss to coat well. 2. Close the lid and move slider to PRESSURE. Make sure the pressure release valve is in the SEAL position. The temperature will default to HIGH, which is the correct setting. Set time to 25 minutes. Select START/STOP to begin cooking. 3. When cooking is complete, naturally release the pressure for 20 minutes. Then turn the pressure relief valve to the VENT position for quick pressure relief. Move slider to AIR FRY/ STOVETOP to unlock the lid, then carefully open it. 4. Shred the meat with two forks in the pot, then stir well until coated with sauce. Set the lid askew over the pot for 5 to 10 minutes to blend the flavours and allow the turkey to continue to absorb the sauce.

Per Serving: Calories 767; Fat 64.69g; Sodium 459mg; Carbs 11.92g; Fibre 1.1g; Sugar 8.03g; Protein 32.39g

Rosemary Balsamic Pulled Chicken

Prep Time: 15 minutes | Cook Time: 20 minutes | Serves: 6

180 ml chicken stock
60 ml balsamic vinegar
60 g strawberry jam (do not use sugar-free)
1 tablespoon Dijon mustard
1 tablespoon ground black pepper, preferably coarsely

ground
1 teaspoon table salt
1.2 kg boneless skinless chicken thighs
1 large rosemary sprig

1. Combine the stock, vinegar, mustard, jam, black pepper, and salt in the pot and stir until the jam dissolves. Add the chicken thighs and toss to coat well. Tuck the rosemary sprig into the mixture. 2. Close the lid and move slider to PRESSURE. Make sure the pressure release valve is in the SEAL position. The temperature will default to HIGH, which is the correct setting. Set time to 20 minutes. 3. When cooking is complete, naturally release the pressure for 10 minutes. Then turn the pressure relief valve to the VENT position for quick pressure relief. Move slider to AIR FRY/ STOVETOP to unlock the lid, then carefully open it. 4. Fish out and discard the rosemary sprig. Shred the meat by two forks in the pot, then stir well to coat with sauce. 5. Set the lid askew over the pot for 5 to 10 minutes to allow the chicken to continue absorbing the sauce.

Per Serving: Calories 302; Fat 7.36g; Sodium 654mg; Carbs 4.52g; Fibre 0.5g; Sugar 3.08g; Protein 50.62g

Simple Buffalo Chicken Wraps

Prep Time: 10 minutes | Cook Time: 12 minutes | Serves: 6

240 ml chicken stock
900 g boneless, skinless chicken breasts
To Serve:

6–8 tortillas, butter lettuce, or your favourite wraps
Buttermilk Ranch Dressing (recipe follows) or bottled

240 g Buffalo sauce of your choice

blue cheese dressing
Blue cheese crumbles for topping (optional)

1. Place the stock and chicken in the pot. 2. Close the lid and move slider to PRESSURE. Make sure the pressure release valve is in the SEAL position. The temperature will default to HIGH, which is the correct setting. Set time to 12 minutes. Select START/STOP to begin cooking. Quick release when done. 3. Transfer the chicken to a bowl, add 60 ml of the cooking liquid from the pot, and shred the chicken using two forks (or a hand mixer to really make it easy). 4. Stir in the Buffalo sauce and serve with your favourite wrap or sandwich fixings. 5. For added zing, top with my Buttermilk Ranch dressing or bottled blue cheese dressing, and sprinkle with blue cheese crumbles.

Per Serving: Calories 614; Fat 19.99g; Sodium 1555mg; Carbs 76.07g; Fibre 3.9g; Sugar 26.08g; Protein 30.63g

Juicy Chicken & Broccoli

Prep Time: 15 minutes | Cook Time: 15 minutes | Serves: 4

680 g chicken, cut into bite-size pieces
1½ tbsp (12 g) cornflour
120 ml coconut aminos or gluten-free tamari
80 ml fresh orange juice
2 tsp (4 g) orange zest
60 ml rice vinegar
2 tsp (10 ml) sesame oil
3 cloves garlic, crushed, divided
1 tbsp (8 g) finely chopped fresh ginger, divided

1 tsp crushed red pepper flakes (optional)
1 tbsp (15 ml) avocado oil
273 g chopped broccoli
740 g cooked quinoa, 744 g rice or 440 g cauliflower rice, for serving
2 tsp (5 g) sesame seeds, for garnish (optional)
2 tbsp (12 g) chopped green onion, for garnish (optional)

1. Place the chicken and cornflour in a resealable plastic bag or lidded plastic container. Shake around until the chicken is well coated. 2. In a bowl, mix together the coconut aminos, vinegar, sesame oil, orange juice and zest, two-thirds of the garlic, two-thirds of the ginger and the red pepper flakes (if using). 3. Move slider to AIR FRY/ STOVETOP. Select SEAR/SAUTÉ and set to 3. Select START/STOP to begin preheating. Allow unit to preheat for 2 minutes. After 2 minutes, add the avocado oil and the remaining garlic and ginger. Stir, then add the chicken. Cook for 1 to 2 minutes, or until the chicken is slightly browned. Press START/STOP to turn off the SEAR/SAUTÉ function. 4. Pour the orange sauce on top of the chicken. 5. Close the lid and move slider to PRESSURE. Make sure the pressure release valve is in the SEAL position. The temperature will default to HIGH, which is the correct setting. Set time to 7 minutes. Select START/STOP to begin cooking. 6. When cooking is complete, turn the pressure relief valve to the VENT position for quick pressure relief. Move slider to the right to unlock the lid, then carefully open it. 7. Toss in the chopped broccoli. Stir, then cook on SEAR/SAUTÉ function and set the heat to 4. Stir and cook the broccoli for another 3 to 4 minutes. 8. Serve over quinoa, rice or cauliflower rice, garnished with the sesame seeds and green onion (if using).

Per Serving: Calories 543; Fat 18.29g; Sodium 155mg; Carbs 48.63g; Fibre 7.4g; Sugar 4.53g; Protein 44.65g

Barbecued Chicken with Simple Slaw

Prep Time: 15 minutes | Cook Time: 20 minutes | Serves: 4

Barbecued Chicken:

½ yellow onion, chopped
1 clove garlic, minced
60 ml raw apple cider vinegar
55 g pure maple syrup
60 ml water
1 tablespoon soy sauce or tamari
455 g boneless, skinless chicken breasts
1 teaspoon fine sea salt

Freshly ground black pepper
60 g tomato paste
1 teaspoon blackstrap molasses
1 teaspoon spicy brown mustard
½ teaspoon chili powder
½ teaspoon paprika
⅛ teaspoon cayenne pepper (optional)
200 g green cabbage, shredded

Simple Slaw:

2 tablespoons freshly squeezed lemon juice
2 tablespoons pure maple syrup
1 tablespoon extra-virgin olive oil
½ teaspoon fine sea salt
Freshly ground black pepper

200 g green cabbage, shredded
1 large shredded carrot (about 1 large carrot)
10 g chopped fresh flat-leaf parsley
Butter lettuce or buns, for serving

1. To make the barbecued chicken, add the onion, garlic, maple syrup, vinegar, water, and soy sauce to the pot and stir to combine well. 2. Then place the bottom layer of the Deluxe Reversible Rack in the lower position in the pot. Place the chicken breasts on the rack. Season the breasts with ¼ teaspoon of the salt and black pepper. 3. Close the lid and move slider to PRESSURE. Make sure the pressure release valve is in the SEAL position. The temperature will default to HIGH, which is the correct setting. Set time to 12 minutes. Select START/STOP to begin cooking. 4. Meanwhile, prepare the slaw. Mix together the lemon juice, maple syrup, olive oil, salt, and several grinds of pepper in a large bowl. Add the carrot, cabbage, and parsley and toss to coat. Refrigerate the slaw to let the flavours meld while you finish preparing the chicken. 5. When cooking is complete, turn the pressure relief valve to the VENT position for quick pressure relief. Move slider to the right to unlock the lid, then carefully open it. 6. Transfer the chicken to a cutting board to rest. Use oven mitts to remove the rack. 7. Move slider to AIR FRY/ STOVETOP. Select SEAR/SAUTÉ and set to 3. Select START/STOP to begin cooking. add the tomato paste, mustard, molasses, paprika, cayenne, chili powder, and the remaining ¾ teaspoon salt to the sauce. Stir well, then add the cabbage. Simmer the cabbage in the sauce until very tender, about 8 minutes. 8. Once the cabbage is tender, use two forks to shred the chicken. Add it to the pot and stir well. Taste and adjust the seasonings as needed; add more cayenne if you like it spicy. 9. To serve, scoop the barbecued chicken into lettuce cups or onto your favourite buns, with the chilled slaw on top. Serve any additional slaw on the side. 10. Store leftovers in two separate airtight containers in the fridge. The chicken will keep for 3 or 4 days, but the slaw is best used within 1 day.
Per Serving: Calories 387; Fat 10.43g; Sodium 1353mg; Carbs 62.5g; Fibre 6.1g; Sugar 34.89g; Protein 13.81g

Delicious Creamy Chicken & Brown Rice

Prep Time: 15 minutes | Cook Time: 25 minutes | Serves: 4

❖ ❖ ❖ ❖ ❖ ❖

1 tablespoon extra-virgin olive oil
1 yellow onion, chopped
200 g cremini mushrooms, roughly chopped
2 cloves garlic, minced
200 g long-grain brown rice, rinsed
300 ml water
1 teaspoon dried thyme

1 teaspoon fine sea salt
455 g boneless, skinless chicken breasts
Freshly ground black pepper
110 g fresh or frozen peas
1 tablespoon freshly squeezed lemon juice
60 ml full-fat canned coconut milk

❖ ❖ ❖ ❖ ❖ ❖

1. Move slider to AIR FRY/STOVETOP. Select SEAR/SAUTÉ and set to 3. Select START/STOP to begin preheating. Allow unit to preheat for 2 minutes. After 2 minutes, add the olive oil to the pot. Once the oil is hot, add the onion, garlic and mushrooms and sauté until softened, about 5 minutes. 2. Add the brown rice, thyme, water, and ½ teaspoon of the salt and stir well, scraping the bottom of the pot with a spatula to make sure nothing has stuck. Place the chicken breasts on top of the rice mixture and season with the remaining ½ teaspoon salt and several grinds of pepper. Press START/STOP to turn off the SEAR/SAUTÉ function. 3. Close the lid and move slider to PRESSURE. Make sure the pressure release valve is in the SEAL position. The temperature will default to HIGH, which is the correct setting. Set time to 10 minutes. Select START/STOP to begin cooking. 4. When cooking is complete, turn the pressure relief valve to the VENT position for quick pressure relief. Move slider to the right to unlock the lid, then carefully open it. 5. Use tongs to transfer the chicken to a cutting board to rest for 5 minutes. If using fresh peas, add them now, scattering them over the rice. Close the lid again, making sure the sealing ring is properly placed. Still cook on high pressure for 8 minutes more. While the rice cooks, cut the chicken into bite-sized pieces. 6. When cooking is complete, naturally release the pressure for 10 minutes. Then turn the pressure relief valve to the VENT position for quick pressure relief. Move slider to AIR FRY/ STOVETOP to unlock the lid, then carefully open it. 7. Stir the chicken into the rice, along with the lemon juice and coconut milk. If using frozen peas, add them now. Taste and adjust the seasoning as needed, then serve immediately. 8. Store the leftovers in an airtight container in the fridge for 3 or 4 days.

Per Serving: Calories 633; Fat 15.94g; Sodium 933mg; Carbs 108.46g; Fibre 11.9g; Sugar 9.3g; Protein 21.37g

Spicy Turkey over Sweet Potato Boats

Prep Time: 25 minutes | Cook Time: 30 minutes | Serves: 4

1 tablespoon extra-virgin olive oil
1 yellow onion, chopped
455 g minced turkey
1 teaspoon chili powder
1½ teaspoons fine sea salt
120 ml water
1 green pepper , seeded and chopped
120 g tomato paste
1 butternut squash (about 455 g), peeled and cut into

2.5 cm cubes, or 200 g frozen butternut squash pieces
2 tablespoons pure maple syrup
1½ tablespoons spicy brown mustard
Freshly ground black pepper
2 small sweet potatoes , pierced with a fork to vent
Chopped green onions, tender white and green parts
only, for garnish
Chopped fresh flat-leaf parsley, for garnish

1. Move slider to AIR FRY/STOVETOP. Select SEAR/SAUTÉ and set to 3. Select START/STOP to begin preheating. Allow unit to preheat for 2 minutes. After 2 minutes, heat the olive oil in the pot. Add the onion, turkey, chili powder, and 1 teaspoon of the salt and sauté until the turkey is browned and cooked through, breaking it up with a wooden spoon as you stir, about 8 minutes. Press START/STOP to turn off the SEAR/SAUTÉ function. 2. Add the water and scrape up any browned bits stuck to the bottom of the pot. Without stirring, add the pepper , butternut squash cubes, maple syrup, tomato paste, mustard, remaining ½ teaspoon salt, and several grinds of pepper. 3. Arrange the Deluxe Reversible Rack on top of the filling and place the sweet potatoes on the rack. 4. Close the lid and move slider to PRESSURE. Make sure the pressure release valve is in the SEAL position. The temperature will default to HIGH, which is the correct setting. Set time to 20 minutes. Select START/STOP to begin cooking. 5. When cooking is complete, naturally release the pressure for 10 minutes. Then turn the pressure relief valve to the VENT position for quick pressure relief. Move slider to AIR FRY/ STOVETOP to unlock the lid, then carefully open it. 6. Use oven mitts to lift the rack and potatoes out of the pot. Stir the filling, using a wooden spoon to mash up the squash. Cook on SEAR/SAUTÉ function and set to 3, simmer away excess liquid until the sauce is to your liking. Adjust the seasoning as needed. 7. Carefully slice the hot sweet potatoes in half lengthwise and spoon filling over each half. Garnish with the green onions and parsley and serve immediately. 8. Store leftover filling in an airtight container in the fridge for 3 or 4 days.

Per Serving: Calories 710; Fat 54.87g; Sodium 1078mg; Carbs 30.01g; Fibre 4.4g; Sugar 17.8g; Protein 25.17g

Chicken Feta Florentine with Spinach

Prep Time: 15 minutes | Cook Time: 15 minutes | Serves: 6

900 g boneless, skinless chicken breasts, sliced crosswise into fillets about 1 cm thick
65 g plain flour (with some garlic powder, salt, and pepper sprinkled in)
60 ml extra-virgin olive oil
4 tablespoons salted butter, divided
1 large shallot, diced
3 cloves garlic, minced or pressed
120 ml dry white wine (like a sauvignon blanc)
Juice of 1 lemon

120 ml garlic stock (e. g. Garlic Better Than Bouillon) or chicken stock
2 teaspoons dried parsley
1 teaspoon salt
1 teaspoon black pepper
200 – 300 g baby spinach
120 g heavy cream
1 package Boursin spread (any flavour) or 100 g cream cheese, cut into chunky cubes
120 g crumbled feta cheese, plus extra for serving

1. Dredge the chicken on both sides in the flour mixture, set aside. 2. Add the olive oil and 2 tablespoons of the butter to the pot. 3. Move slider to AIR FRY/STOVETOP. Select SEAR/SAUTÉ and set to 4. Select START/ STOP to begin cooking. Heat the butter for about 3 minutes. Working in batches so as not to crowd the pot, sear the chicken for 1 minute per side until very lightly browned. Remove from the pot and set aside. 4. Add the remaining 2 tablespoons of butter to the pot, and once it melts, scrape up any browned bits or flour from the bottom of the pot. 5. Add the shallot and sauté for about 2 minutes, until lightly brown, then add the garlic and sauté for another minute. 6. Pour the white wine and lemon juice to the pot and simmer for 1 minute longer. 7. Add the stock, salt , parsley, and pepper. Stir well, scraping the bottom of the pot again, then add the chicken back to the pot and top it off with the spinach, but do not stir. Just lay the spinach on top and push it down gently with your hand. It's going to come to the brim, but don't worry—it will cook down significantly. 8. Close the lid and move slider to PRESSURE. Make sure the pressure release valve is in the SEAL position. The temperature will default to HIGH, which is the correct setting. Set time to 5 minutes. Select START/STOP to begin cooking. Quick release when done. 9. Move the spinach aside and transfer the chicken pieces to a serving dish. Stir the cream, Boursin or cream cheese, and feta into the sauce. To serve, pour the sauce over the chicken and top with extra feta.

Per Serving: Calories 548; Fat 28.27g; Sodium 1204mg; Carbs 49.65g; Fibre 4.7g; Sugar 10.52g; Protein 22.38g

Turkey and Vegetable Stew

Prep Time: 15 minutes | Cook Time: 20 minutes | Serves: 6

675 g lean turkey mince
1 large egg white
2 tablespoons Dijon mustard
2 teaspoons dried sage
½ teaspoon table salt
½ teaspoon ground black pepper
3 tablespoons butter
1 medium yellow onion, chopped
2 medium carrots, thinly sliced

200 g thinly sliced white button mushrooms
2 medium garlic cloves, peeled and minced (2 teaspoons)
1 teaspoon dried thyme
½ teaspoon celery seeds
1 L chicken stock
One can diced tomatoes
1 tablespoon tomato paste
95 g purchased plain croutons

1. In a medium bowl, mix the turkey, mustard, egg white, sage, salt, and pepper, stir until uniform. Set aside. 2. Move slider to AIR FRY/STOVETOP. Select SEAR/SAUTÉ and set to 3. Select START/STOP to begin cooking. 3. Melt the butter in the pot. Add the onion and carrot. Cook, stirring often, until the onion softens, about 3 minutes. Add the mushrooms and cook, stirring more often, until they release their internal moisture and it thickens into a sauce, about 5 minutes. Stir in the garlic, thyme, and celery seeds until aromatic, just a few seconds. 4. Pour in the stock, scrape any browned bits off the pot's bottom. Press START/STOP to turn off the SEAR/SAUTÉ function. Stir in the tomatoes and tomato paste. Drop the turkey mixture in heaping teaspoonsful into the stew. Stir very gently to keep from breaking them up. 5. Close the lid and move slider to PRESSURE. Make sure the pressure release valve is in the SEAL position. The temperature will default to HIGH, which is the correct setting. Set time to 10 minutes. Select START/STOP to begin cooking. 6. When cooking is complete, turn the pressure relief valve to the VENT position for quick pressure relief. Move slider to the right to unlock the lid, then carefully open it. Stir gently. Serve in bowls with the croutons sprinkled on top.

Per Serving: Calories 421; Fat 26.87g; Sodium 1102mg; Carbs 14.24g; Fibre 2.2g; Sugar 3.9g; Protein 31.69g

Prep Time: 15 minutes | Cook Time: 10 minutes | Serves: 4

1 large jarred roasted red pepper
6 sun-dried tomatoes packed in oil
60 ml dry but light red wine, such as Pinot Noir
1 tablespoon mild paprika
½ teaspoon ground cinnamon
½ teaspoon table salt
¼ teaspoon red pepper flakes

2 tablespoons butter
455 g lean turkey mince
One can black-eyed peas, drained and rinsed
One can diced tomatoes
120 ml chicken stock
2 tablespoons loosely packed fresh dill fronds, finely chopped

1. Add the roasted pepper, sun-dried tomatoes, paprika, cinnamon, wine, salt, and red pepper flakes to a food processor. Pulse to create a coarse but thin sauce, stopping the machine at least once to scrape down the inside. 2. Move slider to AIR FRY/STOVETOP. Select SEAR/SAUTÉ and set to 3. Select START/STOP to begin cooking. 3. Melt the butter in the pot. Crumble in the ground turkey and cook, stirring constantly to break up any clumps, until lightly browned, about 4 minutes. Scrape every bit of the red pepper paste into the cooker and cook, stirring all the while, for 1 minute. 4. Press START/STOP to turn off the SEAR/SAUTÉ function. Stir in the black-eyed peas, tomatoes, dill and stock until uniform. 5. Close the lid and move slider to PRESSURE. Make sure the pressure release valve is in the SEAL position. The temperature will default to HIGH, which is the correct setting. Set time to 5 minutes. Select START/STOP to begin cooking. 6. When cooking is complete, turn the pressure relief valve to the VENT position for quick pressure relief. Move slider to the right to unlock the lid, then carefully open it. Stir well before serving.

Per Serving: Calories 470; Fat 21.5g; Sodium 783mg; Carbs 35.5g; Fibre 9.9g; Sugar 9.23g; Protein 37.5g

Juicy Fiesta Chicken Tacos

Prep Time: 15 minutes | Cook Time: 12 minutes | Serves: 6

The Fiesta Chicken:

1 jar red salsa
240 ml chicken stock
60 g taco sauce
1 (25 g) packet taco seasoning

1 teaspoon garlic powder
1 teaspoon Goya sazón seasoning (optional)
900 g boneless, skinless chicken breasts
10–12 tortillas or taco shells

The Taco Fixin'S:

Sour cream
Guacamole

Shredded cheese
Diced tomatoes

1. Mix together the salsa, taco sauce, taco seasoning, chicken stock, garlic powder, and sazón seasoning (if using) in the pot. Add the chicken breasts. 2. Close the lid and move slider to PRESSURE. Make sure the pressure release valve is in the SEAL position. The temperature will default to HIGH, which is the correct setting. Set time to 12 minutes. Select START/STOP to begin cooking. 3. When cooking is complete, turn the pressure relief valve to the VENT position for quick pressure relief. Move slider to the right to unlock the lid, then carefully open it. 4. Transfer the chicken to a bowl and shred it using two forks (or a hand mixer to really make it easy). 5. After the chicken is shredded, mix in as much of the sauce as you'd like to keep the chicken moist and juicy. 6. Serve with tortillas or taco shells and your favourite taco fixings—like sour cream, shredded cheese, guacamole, tomatoes, and more of the fiesta sauce the chicken cooked in.

Per Serving: Calories 591; Fat 27.69g; Sodium 1382mg; Carbs 53.44g; Fibre 5.8g; Sugar 44.54g; Protein 30.94g

Herbed Chicken Breasts with Mushrooms

Prep Time: 15 minutes | Cook Time: 35 minutes | Serves: 4

2 tablespoons butter
Four bone-in skin-on chicken breasts, any rib bits or large hunks of fat removed
½ teaspoon table salt (optional)
½ teaspoon ground black pepper
1 large yellow onion, chopped

200 g thinly sliced white button mushrooms
1 tablespoon dried spice blend, such as herbes de Provence, an Italian blend, a Cajun blend, or even Mrs. Dash
240 ml chicken stock

1. Move slider to AIR FRY/STOVETOP. Select SEAR/SAUTÉ and set to 3. Select START/STOP to begin cooking. Melt the butter in the pot. Season the chicken breasts with the salt (if using) and pepper, then add two of them skin side down to the pot. Brown well without turning, about 5 minutes. 2. Transfer the breasts to a bowl and brown the other two in the same way before transferring them to the bowl. 3. Add the onion and cook, stirring occasionally, until softened, about 4 minutes. Add the mushrooms and cook, stirring more often, until they give off their internal liquid and it reduces to a glaze, about 5 minutes. 4. Stir in the spice blend until aromatic, just a few seconds. Pour in the stock, press START/STOP to turn off the SEAR/SAUTÉ function and scrape up any browned bits on the pot's bottom. Nestle the breasts skin side up in the sauce, overlapping them to fit. 5. Close the lid and move slider to PRESSURE. Make sure the pressure release valve is in the SEAL position. The temperature will default to HIGH, which is the correct setting. Set time to 14 minutes. Select START/STOP to begin cooking. 6. When cooking is complete, turn the pressure relief valve to the VENT position for quick pressure relief. Move slider to the right to unlock the lid, then carefully open it. 7. Use kitchen tongs to transfer the breasts to serving bowls. Spoon the sauce and vegetables over them.

Per Serving: Calories 424; Fat 28.13g; Sodium 1551mg; Carbs 5.47g; Fibre 1g; Sugar 1.51g; Protein 37.22g

Delicious Chicken With Hazelnuts

Prep Time: 15 minutes | Cook Time: 12 minutes | Serves: 6

2 tablespoons olive oil
100 g lean pork mince
60 g skinned hazelnuts, chopped
1 teaspoon ground cinnamon
1 teaspoon ground dried ginger
½ teaspoon table salt
1.2 kg boneless skinless chicken breasts, cut into 1

cm-thick strips
240 ml chicken stock
1 tablespoon honey
Up to ½ teaspoon red pepper flakes
Up to ¼ teaspoon saffron
1 tablespoon fresh lemon juice

1. Move slider to AIR FRY/STOVETOP. Select SEAR/SAUTÉ and set to 3. Select START/STOP to begin cooking. 2. Warm the oil in the pot for a minute or two. Crumble in the ground pork and cook, stirring frequently to break up any clumps, until lightly browned, about 4 minutes. Add the hazelnuts, ginger, cinnamon, and salt, stirring until fragrant, for about 30 seconds. 3. Add the chicken and stir until evenly coated. Press START/STOP to turn off the SEAR/SAUTÉ function. Scrape up any browned bits on the pot's bottom. Stir in the honey, red pepper flakes, and saffron. 4. Close the lid and move slider to PRESSURE. Make sure the pressure release valve is in the SEAL position. The temperature will default to HIGH, which is the correct setting. Set time to 5 minutes. Select START/STOP to begin cooking. 5. When cooking is complete, turn the pressure relief valve to the VENT position for quick pressure relief. Move slider to the right to unlock the lid, then carefully open it. 6. Stir in the lemon juice before serving.

Per Serving: Calories 437; Fat 19.84g; Sodium 459mg; Carbs 5.87g; Fibre 1.4g; Sugar 3.45g; Protein 56.91g

Prep Time: 15 minutes | Cook Time: 35 minutes | Serves: 4

2 tablespoons olive oil
Four bone-in skin-on chicken breasts
1 medium yellow onion, chopped
1 medium red pepper , stemmed, cored, and cut into thin strips
1 medium green pepper , stemmed, cored, and cut into thin strips
1 medium yellow pepper , stemmed, cored, and cut into thin strips

3 medium garlic cloves, peeled and minced (1 tablespoon)
1 tablespoon packed fresh rosemary leaves, minced
1 tablespoon packed fresh oregano leaves, minced
1 to 2 jarred anchovy fillets, finely chopped
¼ teaspoon table salt
2 tablespoons balsamic vinegar
300 ml chicken stock

1. Move slider to AIR FRY/STOVETOP. Select SEAR/SAUTÉ and set to 3. Select START/STOP to begin preheating. Allow unit to preheat for 2 minutes. 2. After 2 minutes, warm the oil for a minute in the pot. Add two of the chicken breasts skin side down and brown well without turning, about 5 minutes. Transfer the breasts to a bowl and brown the other two in the same way before transferring them to the bowl. 3. Add the onion and all the pepper strips. Cook, stirring occasionally, until softened, about 4 minutes. Stir in the garlic, oregano, rosemary, anchovies, and salt until aromatic, just a few seconds. 4. Pour in the vinegar and scrape up any browned bits on the pot's bottom. Press START/STOP to turn off the SEAR/SAUTÉ function. Pour in the stock and stir well. Nestle the chicken breasts skin side up in the sauce; drizzle any juice from their bowl over them. 5. Close the lid and move slider to PRESSURE. Make sure the pressure release valve is in the SEAL position. The temperature will default to HIGH, which is the correct setting. Set time to 16 minutes. Select START/STOP to begin cooking. 6. When cooking is complete, turn the pressure relief valve to the VENT position for quick pressure relief. Move slider to the right to unlock the lid, then carefully open it. 7. Transfer the chicken breasts to serving plates or a serving platter. Spoon some of the sauce over them before serving.

Per Serving: Calories 218; Fat 12.1g; Sodium 827mg; Carbs 9.25g; Fibre 1.5g; Sugar 4.82g; Protein 17.77

Balsamic Beef Roast with Potatoes & Carrots

Prep Time: 15 minutes | Cook Time: 55 minutes | Serves: 6

1.8 kg chuck beef roast, cut into 4 pieces, fat trimmed
2 tsp (12 g) sea salt, plus more to taste
1 tsp paprika
1 tsp dried rosemary
1 tsp dried basil
1 tsp dried thyme
1 tsp onion powder
1 tsp garlic powder
3 tbsp (45 ml) olive or avocado oil

1 small yellow onion, diced
237 ml cabernet sauvignon wine
355 ml beef stock
60 ml balsamic vinegar
2 tbsp (30 ml) gluten-free tamari or coconut aminos
4 large carrots, peeled and cut into 5- to 7.5-cm pieces
340 g sliced bella mushrooms or button mushrooms
680 g baby potatoes
3 tbsp (24 g) tapioca starch

1. Pat the beef dry. In a medium bowl, combine together the salt, paprika, basil, thyme, rosemary, onion powder and garlic powder. Generously rub the mixture on all sides of the beef pieces. 2. Move slider to AIR FRY/STOVETOP. Select SEAR/SAUTÉ and set to 3. Select START/STOP to begin cooking. Add oil to the pot, heat the oil for 1 minute and then toss in the onion. Cook for 2 minutes, then add the meat, a few pieces at a time. Cook for about 2 minutes per side, and repeat until all of the pieces have been seared. Press START/STOP to turn off the SEAR/ SAUTÉ function. Remove the beef from the pot and set aside. 3. Deglaze the pot by pouring in the wine and beef stock. Scrape the bottom for any leftover browned bits. Pour in the vinegar and gluten-free tamari. Place the beef on top of the liquid mixture, then top with the carrots, mushrooms and potatoes. 4. Close the lid and move slider to PRESSURE. Make sure the pressure release valve is in the SEAL position. The temperature will default to HIGH, which is the correct setting. Set time to 40 minutes. Select START/STOP to begin cooking. 5. When cooking is complete, naturally release the pressure for 10 minutes. Then turn the pressure relief valve to the VENT position for quick pressure relief. Move slider to AIR FRY/ STOVETOP to unlock the lid, then carefully open it. 6. Gently remove the vegetables and then the beef. Set both aside separately, tented with foil to keep warm. 7. Transfer about 60 ml of the cooking liquid into a small bowl, whisk in the tapioca starch, then return the liquid to the pot and stir. Cook on SEAR/SAUTÉ function and set the heat to 4, and allow the sauce to thicken, 5 to 7 minutes. 8. While the sauce is cooking, shred or cut the beef. Place back in the pot. Spoon the beef and sauce over the vegetables and serve warm.

Per Serving: Calories 822; Fat 34.32g; Sodium 1183mg; Carbs 36.39g; Fibre 5.1g; Sugar 7.1g; Protein 86.81g

Apple Cider–Braised Kielbasa Sausage with Carrots & Potatoes

Prep Time: 15 minutes | Cook Time: 25 minutes | Serves: 2

1 teaspoon oil
225 g uncooked thick-cut bacon, chopped
225 g fully cooked kielbasa sausage, cut into 5 cm pieces
1 onion, chopped
2 garlic cloves, minced
1 bay leaf
½ teaspoon dried tarragon

Salt
Freshly ground black pepper
2 medium potatoes, quartered and thickly sliced
2 carrots, peeled and chopped
240 ml apple cider
1 teaspoon ham bouillon powder
10 g chopped fresh parsley

1. Move slider to AIR FRY/STOVETOP. Select SEAR/SAUTÉ and set to 3. Select START/STOP to begin preheating. Allow unit to preheat for 2 minutes. After 2 minutes, add the oil. Add the bacon and kielbasa and sauté until crisp and brown, 3 to 5 minutes. Transfer to a plate and set aside. 2. Add the onion to the rendered bacon fat in the pot and sauté until softened, 3 to 4 minutes. Add the garlic, bay leaf, and tarragon and sauté for 1 minute. Season with salt and pepper. 3. Add the potatoes and carrots, then return the bacon and sausage to the pot. Stir in the apple cider and ham bouillon powder. 4. Close the lid and move slider to PRESSURE. Make sure the pressure release valve is in the SEAL position. The temperature will default to HIGH, which is the correct setting. Set time to 12 minutes. Select START/STOP to begin cooking. When the timer beeps, quick release the pressure to naturally release for 5 minutes. Open the lid. 5. Discard the bay leaf. Taste and season with more salt and pepper if needed. Divide between serving bowls and garnish with the parsley.

Per Serving: Calories 949; Fat 46.9g; Sodium 1526mg; Carbs 88.77g; Fibre 12.3g; Sugar 15.27g; Protein 46.59g

Smoked BBQ Beef Brisket

Prep Time: 15 minutes | Cook Time: 50 minutes | Serves: 4

900 g. beef brisket, flat cut
¼ tsp garlic salt
¼ tsp celery salt
1 tsp seasoned meat tenderizer

2 tbsp liquid smoke
1 tbsp Worcestershire sauce
120 ml water
160 g BBQ sauce, plus additional for serving

1. Mix together the garlic salt, celery salt and seasoned meat tenderizer in a large bowl. 2. In the same bowl, rub all sides of the beef brisket with the spice mix. Pour the Worcestershire sauce and liquid smoke over the brisket. 3. Cover the bowl tightly with aluminum foil and let marinate for at least 45 minutes or up to 9 hours in the refrigerator. 4. Pour the water and BBQ sauce into the pot. 5. Add the brisket and remaining liquid from the bowl to the pot. 6. Close the lid and move slider to PRESSURE. Make sure the pressure release valve is in the SEAL position. The temperature will default to HIGH, which is the correct setting. Set time to 50 minutes. Select START/STOP to begin cooking. 7. When cooking is complete, naturally release the pressure for 15 minutes. Then turn the pressure relief valve to the VENT position for quick pressure relief. Move slider to AIR FRY/ STOVETOP to unlock the lid, then carefully open it. 8. Transfer the brisket to a serving plate. Slice the meat and serve with additional BBQ sauce.

Per Serving: Calories 468; Fat 33.89g; Sodium 1855mg; Carbs 4.3g; Fibre 0.9g; Sugar 2.14g; Protein 34.15g

Pork Stroganoff with Noodles

Prep Time: 15 minutes | Cook Time: 20 minutes | Serves: 6

900 g pork loin, cut into 1 cm strips
1 tbsp olive oil
½ tsp salt
½ tsp ground black pepper
1 onion, chopped
3 carrots, chopped

2 stalks of celery, chopped
480 ml chicken stock
1 tbsp flour
1 tbsp Dijon mustard
120 g sour cream
1 package egg noodles, cooked

1. Move slider to AIR FRY/STOVETOP. Select SEAR/SAUTÉ and set to 3. Select START/STOP to begin preheating. Allow unit to preheat for 2 minutes. After 2 minutes, heat the oil in the pot. 2. Season the meat with salt and pepper and put into the pot. 3. Cook until all the meat is browned. You may do it in two batches. 4. Remove the pork from the pot. Add the onion and sauté for 3 minutes. 5. Pour in 240 ml of stock and deglaze the pot by scraping the bottom to remove all of the brown bits. 6. Add the carrots and celery. 7. In a bowl, combine 240 ml of stock, flour and Dijon mustard. 8. Pour the mixture in the pot. Stir well and bring to a boil. 9. Press START/STOP to turn off the SEAR/SAUTÉ function. 10. Return the meat to the pot. Close the lid. Move slider to PRESSURE. Make sure the pressure release valve is in the SEAL position. The temperature will default to HIGH, which is the correct setting. Set time to 7 minutes. Select START/STOP to begin cooking. 11. When the timer beeps, use a natural release for 10 minutes, then release any remaining pressure manually. Open the lid. 12. Move slider to AIR FRY/STOVETOP. Select SEAR/SAUTÉ and set to Lo1. Select START/STOP to begin cooking. Add the sour cream and mix well. Simmer for 1 minute. Press the START/STOP button to stop the SEAR/SAUTÉ function. 13. Serve the meat with the sauce and cooked noodles.
Per Serving: Calories 409; Fat 21.58g; Sodium 657mg; Carbs 10.4g; Fibre 1.6g; Sugar 2.95g; Protein 41.18g

Cheese Meatballs with Spaghetti

Prep Time: 15 minutes | Cook Time: 15 minutes | Serves: 2

115 g beef mince
115 g pork mince
2 slices white bread
25 g grated Parmesan cheese
1 large egg
1 garlic clove, minced
½ teaspoon dried oregano

½ tablespoon dried parsley
Pinch salt
Pinch freshly ground black pepper
Oil, for shaping the meatballs
720 g easy marinara sauce, divided
150 g spaghetti
240 ml beef stock

1. In a medium bowl, put the minced beef and pork. Dampen the bread with water, gently squeeze the excess water out, then crumble over the meat. Whisk in the egg, cheese, garlic, parsley, oregano, salt, and pepper. Coat your hands with a bit of the oil, mix the meat together well by hand, and roll into tablespoon-size balls, setting them aside on a plate as you work. Refrigerate for 20 minutes. 2. Add half of the marinara sauce to the pot. Place the meatballs on top in an even layer. Cover the meatballs with another thin layer of sauce. Break the spaghetti in half and lay on top of the meatballs. Pour the remaining sauce on top, then add the beef stock. 3. Close the lid and move slider to PRESSURE. Make sure the pressure release valve is in the SEAL position. The temperature will default to HIGH, which is the correct setting. Set time to 15 minutes. Select START/STOP to begin cooking. 4. When cooking is complete, turn the pressure relief valve to the VENT position for quick pressure relief. Move slider to the right to unlock the lid, then carefully open it. 5. Stir the contents of the pot, breaking apart any noodles stuck together. Divide the spaghetti and meatballs between two bowls or plates and serve with grated Parmesan and garlic bread.
Per Serving: Calories 800; Fat 35.83g; Sodium 1032mg; Carbs 70.15g; Fibre 13.5g; Sugar 24.02g; Protein 49.25g

Homemade Potato Meatloaf

Prep Time: 15 minutes | Cook Time: 30 minutes | Serves: 6

675 g lean beef mince
One 200 g russet or baking potato, peeled and shredded through the large holes of a box grater
25 g plain panko breadcrumbs
1 large egg
2 tablespoons Worcestershire sauce
2 tablespoons ketchup
1 teaspoon dried oregano

1 teaspoon dried thyme
1 teaspoon onion powder
½ teaspoon garlic powder
1 teaspoon table salt
½ teaspoon ground black pepper
Olive oil spray
360 ml water

1. In a large bowl, mix together the minced meat, potato, breadcrumbs, egg, ketchup, oregano, thyme, onion powder, Worcestershire sauce, garlic powder, salt, and pepper until uniform. 2. Generously coat the inside of a baking pan that fits the pot with olive oil spray. Pack the minced beef mixture into this pan, creating an even, smooth layer. Cover the pan with aluminum foil; poke a fairly large hole in the centre of the foil where the hole exists in the centre post of the pan. 3. Pour the water into the pot. Then place the bottom layer of the Deluxe Reversible Rack in the lower position in the pot. Set the covered pan on the rack. 4. Close the lid and move slider to PRESSURE. Make sure the pressure release valve is in the SEAL position. The temperature will default to HIGH, which is the correct setting. Set time to 30 minutes. Select START/STOP to begin cooking. 5. When cooking is complete, naturally release the pressure for 20 minutes. Then turn the pressure relief valve to the VENT position for quick pressure relief. Move slider to AIR FRY/ STOVETOP to unlock the lid, then carefully open it. 6. Poke an instant-read meat thermometer through the foil and into the centre of the loaf without touching metal in at least two places to make sure the meatloaf's temperature is 75°C. If it is not, cook for another 5 minutes. 7. Once done, use the handle of a wooden spoon leveraged into the centre hole of the baking pan (also wear oven mitts) to transfer the hot pan to a wire rack. Cool for a few minutes, just until you can handle the pan. 8. Using oven mitts, tip the pan a bit this way and that over a trash can to pour off any juices around the meatloaf. Set a platter over the pan, invert the whole thing (watch out for more hot juices!), and remove the pan. Cool for a few more minutes before slicing.
Per Serving: Calories 374; Fat 19.95g; Sodium 596mg; Carbs 13.83g; Fibre 2.2g; Sugar 3.08g; Protein 34.06g

Chinese Water Chestnuts Meatballs

Prep Time: 15 minutes | Cook Time: 10 minutes | Serves: 4

455 g lean minced beef
One 200 g can whole or sliced water chestnuts, drained and chopped
1 large egg white
2 tablespoons dry sherry, dry vermouth, or dry white wine
1 tablespoon minced peeled fresh ginger

60 ml plus 1 tablespoon unseasoned rice vinegar
1 teaspoon five-spice powder
½ teaspoon ground black pepper
200 g raw short-grain white rice
240 ml water
60 ml soy sauce
60 ml Worcestershire sauce

1. In a medium bowl, mix the beef, water chestnuts, sherry, egg white, ginger, the five-spice powder, 1 tablespoon vinegar, and pepper until uniform. Form this mixture into 18 balls, each about the size of a golf ball, made from about 2 tablespoons of the mixture. 2. Pour the rice on a large plate, platter, or cutting board. Roll the balls in the rice, getting the grains to adhere evenly all over each ball. 3. Pour the water into the pot. Then place the bottom layer of the Cook & Crisp Basket in the lower position in the pot. Pile the balls into the basket and close the lid. 4. Move slider to PRESSURE. Make sure the pressure release valve is in the SEAL position. The temperature will default to HIGH, which is the correct setting. Set time to 10 minutes. Select START/STOP to begin cooking. 5. Meanwhile, whisk the Worcestershire sauce, soy sauce, and the remaining 60 ml rice vinegar in a small bowl. Set aside. 6. When cooking is complete, naturally release the pressure for 10 minutes. Then turn the pressure relief valve to the VENT position for quick pressure relief. Move slider to AIR FRY/ STOVETOP to unlock the lid, then carefully open it. 7. Lift the hot basket out of the cooker or gently transfer the balls one by one to a serving platter with kitchen tongs. Serve with the dipping sauce on the side.
Per Serving: Calories 525; Fat 15.9g; Sodium 500mg; Carbs 56.06g; Fibre 2.8g; Sugar 10.78g; Protein 36.09g

Easy Feta Beef Stew

Prep Time: 15 minutes | Cook Time: 40 minutes | Serves: 6

1.3 kg beef shoulder, cut into chunks
1 tsp sea salt
½ tsp ground black pepper
240 ml beef stock
1 tsp red wine vinegar
55 g sun-dried tomatoes
1 onion, sliced

5 cloves garlic, minced
1 tbsp oregano
½ tsp marjoram
1 tbsp dried basil
1 tsp dill
60 g feta cheese, crumbled

1. Dump all of the ingredients, except the feta cheese, into the pot and stir to mix everything evenly. 2. Close the lid and move slider to PRESSURE. Make sure the pressure release valve is in the SEAL position. The temperature will default to HIGH, which is the correct setting. Set time to 40 minutes. Select START/STOP to begin cooking. 3. When cooking is complete, naturally release the pressure for 10 minutes. Then turn the pressure relief valve to the VENT position for quick pressure relief. Move slider to AIR FRY/ STOVETOP to unlock the lid, then carefully open it. 4. Top with feta cheese and serve.
Per Serving: Calories 350; Fat 13.77g; Sodium 783mg; Carbs 5.51g; Fibre 1.1g; Sugar 2.91g; Protein 52.3g

Red Wine Braised Lamb with Tomatoes

Prep Time: 15 minutes | Cook Time: 1⅔ hours | Serves: 8

◆ ◆ ◆ ◆ ◆ ◆

2 tablespoons olive oil
One 1.2 – 1.7 kg boneless leg of lamb
1 teaspoon table salt
½ teaspoon ground black pepper
240 ml dry, light red wine, such as Pinot Noir
120 ml chicken stock

1 medium yellow onion, peeled and halved
4 whole cloves
3 medium Roma or plum tomatoes, chopped
2 large carrots, cut into 5 cm sections
6 large garlic cloves, peeled
2 teaspoon dried thyme

◆ ◆ ◆ ◆ ◆ ◆

1. Move slider to AIR FRY/STOVETOP. Select SEAR/SAUTÉ and set to 3. Select START/STOP to begin preheating. Allow unit to preheat for 2 minutes. 2. After 2 minutes, warm the oil in the pot for a minute or two. Season the lamb with the salt and pepper, then place it in the pot and brown well on all sides, even the ends, turning occasionally, about 12 minutes. Transfer the leg of lamb to a nearby bowl. 3. Pour in the wine and stock, then scrape off any browned bits from the bottom of the pot. Press START/STOP to turn off the SEAR/SAUTÉ function. Stud the onion pieces with the whole cloves; add these to the pot and then add the carrots, tomatoes, garlic, and thyme. Return the lamb to the pot. 4. Close the lid and move slider to PRESSURE. Make sure the pressure release valve is in the SEAL position. Set the temperature to LOW and set time to 1 hour and 30 minutes. Select START/STOP to begin cooking. 5. When cooking is complete, naturally release the pressure for 25 minutes. Then turn the pressure relief valve to the VENT position for quick pressure relief. Move slider to AIR FRY/ STOVETOP to unlock the lid, then carefully open it. 6. Transfer the leg of lamb to a clean cutting board. 7. Fish out and discard the onions, carrots, and the cloves that have slipped off the onions. Use an immersion blender right in the cooker to blend the remaining ingredients in the pot into a sauce—or pour the contents of the insert into a blender, cover, remove the centre knob, cover the hole with a clean kitchen towel, and blend until smooth. 8. To serve, carve the meat into 2.5 cm slices and/or chunks, then serve them with the sauce ladled on top.
Per Serving: Calories 233; Fat 9.47g; Sodium 450mg; Carbs 15.96g; Fibre 2.3g; Sugar 11.62g; Protein 21.41g

Herbed Cumin Beef Brisket

Prep Time: 15 minutes | Cook Time: 60 minutes | Serves: 6

◆ ◆ ◆ ◆ ◆ ◆

1.3 kg. beef brisket, flat cut
60 ml soy sauce
¼ tsp salt
1 tbsp dried coriander
1 tsp ground cinnamon

½ tbsp dried oregano
1 tbsp ground cumin
1½ tbsp dried rosemary
360 ml beef stock

◆ ◆ ◆ ◆ ◆ ◆

1. In a bowl, mix together the soy sauce, coriander, cinnamon, salt, cumin, oregano, and rosemary. 2. Rub all sides of the brisket with the spice mix. 3. Let marinate for at least 45 minutes or up to 9 hours in the refrigerator. 4. Add the beef brisket to the pot. Add the beef stock. 5. Close the lid and move slider to PRESSURE. Make sure the pressure release valve is in the SEAL position. The temperature will default to HIGH, which is the correct setting. Set time to 60 minutes. 6. Select START/STOP to begin cooking. 7. When cooking is complete, naturally release the pressure for 10 minutes. Then turn the pressure relief valve to the VENT position for quick pressure relief. Move slider to AIR FRY/ STOVETOP to unlock the lid, then carefully open it. 8. Transfer the meat to a plate and slice it. Serve.
Per Serving: Calories 494; Fat 36.04g; Sodium 1438mg; Carbs 4.88g; Fibre 0.8g; Sugar 2.42g; Protein 35.49g

Braised Short Ribs with Mushrooms

2 thin strips of bacon, chopped
2½ tablespoons butter, 1½ tablespoons of it at room temperature
1.4 kg boneless beef short ribs
1 small red onion, chopped
455 g thinly sliced brown cremini mushrooms
240 ml dry red wine

120 ml beef or chicken stock
2 teaspoons dried thyme
1 teaspoon dried sage
½ teaspoon table salt
½ teaspoon ground black pepper
2 bay leaves
1½ tablespoons plain flour

1. Move slider to AIR FRY/STOVETOP. Select SEAR/SAUTÉ and set to 3. Select START/STOP to begin preheating. Allow unit to preheat for 2 minutes. 2. After 2 minutes, melt 1 tablespoon butter in the pot. Add the bacon and fry until crisp, stirring occasionally, about 4 minutes. Use a slotted spoon to transfer the bacon to a nearby bowl. 3. Add half the short ribs and brown them well on all sides, turning occasionally, about 10 minutes. Transfer these to that bowl and add the remaining short ribs, browning them in just the same way. Transfer these to the bowl, too. 4. Add the onion and cook, stirring frequently, until softened, about 3 minutes. Add the mushrooms and continue cooking, stirring occasionally, until they give off their internal moisture and that liquid evaporates to a glaze in the pot, about 5 minutes. 5. Pour in the wine and scrape up the browned bits on the pot's bottom. Press START/STOP to turn off the SEAR/SAUTÉ function. Stir in the stock, sage, thyme, salt, pepper, and bay leaves. Return the short ribs, bacon, and any juices in that bowl to the pot. Stir well. 6. Close the lid and move slider to PRESSURE. Make sure the pressure release valve is in the SEAL position. Set the temperature to LOW and set time to 1 hour and 30 minutes. Select START/STOP to begin cooking. 7. When cooking is complete, naturally release the pressure for 30 minutes. Then turn the pressure relief valve to the VENT position for quick pressure relief. Move slider to AIR FRY/ STOVETOP to unlock the lid, then carefully open it. 8. Unlatch the lid and open the cooker. Find and discard the bay leaves. Use kitchen tongs and a slotted spoon to transfer the short ribs, bacon, and any vegetables to a serving platter. Tent with aluminum foil to keep warm. Use a flatware tablespoon to skim any excess surface fat from the sauce in the pot. 9. Move slider to AIR FRY/STOVETOP. Select SEAR/SAUTÉ and set to 3. Select START/STOP to begin cooking. 10. As the sauce comes to a simmer, use a fork to make a smooth paste out of the flour and the remaining, room-temperature 1½ tablespoons butter in a small bowl. 11. As the sauce simmers, whisk this flour mixture into the pot in dribs and drabs, just a little at a time, whisking until it's all been added and the sauce has thickened, 1 to 2 minutes. 12. Turn off the SEAR/SAUTÉ function and pour the sauce in the hot pot over the meat and vegetables on the platter.

Per Serving: Calories 731; Fat 49.61g; Sodium 635mg; Carbs 3.53g; Fibre 0.5g; Sugar 0.79g; Protein 66.59g

Tea–Braised Eye of Round Roast with Leek

Prep Time: 15 minutes | Cook Time: 1⅔ hours | Serves: 8

480 ml water
60 ml loose Lapsang Souchong tea or 6 Lapsang Souchong tea bags, any labels removed
2 tablespoons vegetable, corn, or canola oil
One 1.3 kg beef eye of round roast
1 teaspoon ground dried ginger

1 teaspoon Sichuan peppercorns (optional)
½ teaspoon table salt
1 medium leek, white and pale green part only, halved lengthwise, washed well, and thinly sliced
1 small fresh serrano chile, stemmed, halved lengthwise, seeded (if desired), and thinly sliced

1. Bring the water to a boil in a medium saucepan set over high heat. Remove the pan from the heat and stir in the loose tea or add the tea bags. Cover and set aside until very dark, about 10 minutes. Strain the tea into a medium bowl or remove and discard the bags. 2. Move slider to AIR FRY/STOVETOP. Select SEAR/SAUTÉ and set to 3. Select START/STOP to begin preheating. Allow unit to preheat for 2 minutes. 3. After 2 minutes, warm the oil in the pot for a minute or two. Add the beef and brown it well on all sides, turning occasionally, about 10 minutes. Transfer the meat to a nearby cutting board. Pour the tea into the pot and stir to get up all the browned bits on the pot's bottom. 4. Press START/STOP to turn off the SEAR/SAUTÉ function; stir in the ginger, Sichuan peppercorns (if using), and salt. Return the roast to the pot. Add the leeks and chile, making sure these are mostly in the stock. 5. Close the lid and move slider to PRESSURE. Make sure the pressure release valve is in the SEAL position. Set the temperature to LOW and set time to 1 hour and 15 minutes. Select START/STOP to begin cooking. 6. When cooking is complete, naturally release the pressure for 30 minutes. Then turn the pressure relief valve to the VENT position for quick pressure relief. Move slider to AIR FRY/ STOVETOP to unlock the lid, then carefully open it. 7. Transfer the roast to a cutting board and cool for 5 minutes. Carve into 1 cm-thick slices and serve in bowls with lots of the stock from the pot.
Per Serving: Calories 324; Fat 11.36g; Sodium 269mg; Carbs 1.83g; Fibre 0.3g; Sugar 0.48g; Protein 50.66g

Spiced Pork Strips with Lettuce

Prep Time: 15 minutes | Cook Time: 40 minutes | Serves: 4

900 g. pork tenderloin, cut into 5 cm strips
3 tbsp garlic, chopped
2 tbsp dried oregano
½ tbsp ground cumin
3 tbsp sweet paprika

½ tsp salt
½ tsp ground black pepper
2 tbsp olive oil
480 ml vegetable stock
90 g lettuce, chopped

1. Mix the garlic, paprika, oregano, cumin, salt and pepper in a large bowl. 2. Rub the pork strips all over until well coated. Let marinate for at least 30 minutes. 3. Move slider to AIR FRY/STOVETOP. Select SEAR/SAUTÉ and set to 3. Select START/STOP to begin preheating. Allow unit to preheat for 2 minutes. After 2 minutes, add and heat the oil. 4. Add the meat and cook for 10 minutes until browned. 5. Pour in the vegetable stock and stir well. Press START/STOP to turn off the SEAR/SAUTÉ function. 6. Close the lid and move slider to PRESSURE. Make sure the pressure release valve is in the SEAL position. The temperature will default to HIGH, which is the correct setting. Set time to 30 minutes. Select START/STOP to begin cooking. 7. When cooking is complete, naturally release the pressure for 15 minutes. Then turn the pressure relief valve to the VENT position for quick pressure relief. Move slider to AIR FRY/ STOVETOP to unlock the lid, then carefully open it. 8. Serve the cooked pork with the chopped lettuce.
Per Serving: Calories 472; Fat 16.83g; Sodium 713mg; Carbs 16.11g; Fibre 5.2g; Sugar 3.27g; Protein 63.84g

Teriyaki Flank Steak with Mushroom & Carrots

Prep Time: 15 minutes | Cook Time: 1¼ hours | Serves: 6

2 tablespoons peanut or toasted sesame oil
One 900 g – 1.1 kg beef flank steak, cut in half widthwise
10 medium spring onions, trimmed and cut into 5 cm pieces
200 g shiitake mushrooms, the stems discarded and the caps thinly sliced

2 medium garlic cloves, peeled and minced (2 teaspoons)
2 tablespoons minced peeled fresh ginger
360 ml beef or chicken stock
2 tablespoons soy sauce
2 tablespoons dark brown sugar
3 medium carrots, cut into 2.5 cm chunks

1. Move slider to AIR FRY/STOVETOP. Select SEAR/SAUTÉ and set to 3. Select START/STOP to begin preheating. Allow unit to preheat for 2 minutes. 2. After 2 minutes, warm 1 tablespoon oil in the pot for 1 to 2 minutes. Add one piece of flank steak and brown it on both sides, turning occasionally, about 8 minutes. Transfer the steak to a nearby cutting board, add the remaining 1 tablespoon oil, and brown the second piece of flank steak in the same way before getting it to the cutting board. 3. Add the spring onions, garlic, mushrooms, and ginger to the pot. Cook, stirring frequently, until the mushrooms begin to soften, about 2 minutes. Pour in the stock and scrape up any browned bits on the pot's bottom. 4. Press START/STOP to turn off the SEAR/SAUTÉ function, then stir in the soy sauce and brown sugar until dissolved. Return the meat and any juices to the pot. Put the carrots on top and close the lid. 5. Move slider to PRESSURE. Make sure the pressure release valve is in the SEAL position. Set the temperature to LOW and set time to 1 hour and 5 minutes. Select START/STOP to begin cooking. 6. When cooking is complete, naturally release the pressure for 30 minutes. Then turn the pressure relief valve to the VENT position for quick pressure relief. Move slider to AIR FRY/ STOVETOP to unlock the lid, then carefully open it. 7. Transfer the meat to a clean cutting board. Slice the meat against the grain into 1 cm-thick slices and serve in bowls with the sauce and carrots.
Per Serving: Calories 219; Fat 9.63g; Sodium 379mg; Carbs 15.42g; Fibre 2.5g; Sugar 7.73g; Protein 18.41g

Delicious Pork Chops with Apples

Prep Time: 15 minutes | Cook Time: 15 minutes | Serves: 4

1 tsp nutmeg
1 tsp cinnamon
4 tbsp brown sugar
2 apples, sliced

4 tbsp butter
4 pork chops, 2 – 2.5 cm thick
Salt and ground black pepper to taste

1. Mix the nutmeg, cinnamon and brown sugar in a bowl. 2. Season the sliced apples with this mix and stir to coat well. 3. Move slider to AIR FRY/STOVETOP. Select SEAR/SAUTÉ and set to 3. Select START/STOP to begin preheating. Allow unit to preheat for 2 minutes. After 2 minutes, add the butter and melt it. 4. Add the apples to the pot and sauté, stirring occasionally, for 2 minutes. 5. Rub both sides of the pork chops with salt and pepper. 6. Put the pork on the apples. Press START/STOP to turn off the SEAR/SAUTÉ function. 7. Close the lid and move slider to PRESSURE. Make sure the pressure release valve is in the SEAL position. The temperature will default to HIGH, which is the correct setting. Set time to 10 minutes. Select START/ STOP to begin cooking. 8. Once the timer beeps, turn the pressure relief valve to the VENT position for quick pressure relief. Move slider to the right to unlock the lid, then carefully open it. Serve.
Per Serving: Calories 517; Fat 29.27g; Sodium 180mg; Carbs 22.42g; Fibre 2.8g; Sugar 17.89g; Protein 40.85g

Country-Style Pork Ribs with Apple Sauce

Prep Time: 15 minutes | Cook Time: 50 minutes | Serves: 6

◆ ◆ ◆ ◆ ◆ ◆

2 tablespoons olive oil
6 bone-in country-style pork ribs
1 medium red onion, chopped
240 ml unsweetened apple cider
70 g chopped dried apples
120 ml chicken stock

1 tablespoon Dijon mustard
2 teaspoons dark brown sugar
1 teaspoon dried sage
1 teaspoon dried thyme
½ teaspoon table salt

◆ ◆ ◆ ◆ ◆ ◆

1. Move slider to AIR FRY/STOVETOP. Select SEAR/SAUTÉ and set to 3. Select START/STOP to begin preheating. Allow unit to preheat for 2 minutes. 2. After 2 minutes, warm the oil in the pot for a minute or two. Add half the country-style ribs and brown well on all sides, turning occasionally, about 8 minutes. Transfer the meat to a nearby bowl and brown the remaining country-style ribs in the same way before getting them into that bowl. 3. Add the onion and cook, stirring frequently, until softened, about 3 minutes. Pour in the cider, Press START/STOP to turn off the SEAR/SAUTÉ function. Scrape up any browned bits on the pot's bottom. Stir in the dried apples, stock, brown sugar, mustard, thyme, sage, and salt. Nestle the ribs into the sauce; add any juice from their bowl. 4. Close the lid and move slider to PRESSURE. Make sure the pressure release valve is in the SEAL position. The temperature will default to HIGH, which is the correct setting. Set time to 35 minutes. Select START/STOP to begin cooking. 5. When cooking is complete, naturally release the pressure for 25 minutes. Then turn the pressure relief valve to the VENT position for quick pressure relief. Move slider to AIR FRY/ STOVETOP to unlock the lid, then carefully open it. 6. Use kitchen tongs to transfer the country-style ribs to a serving platter. Use a flatware tablespoon to skim any excess surface fat from the sauce. 7. Move slider to AIR FRY/STOVETOP. Select SEAR/ SAUTÉ and set to Hi5. Select START/STOP to begin cooking. 8. Bring the sauce in the pot to a boil. Cook, stirring frequently, until reduced to half its original volume, about 5 minutes. Turn off the SEAR/SAUTÉ function. Serve the country-style ribs with lots of the sauce drizzled over them—and more on the side for dipping.

Per Serving: Calories 377; Fat 17.16g; Sodium 438mg; Carbs 7.39g; Fibre 1.1g; Sugar 5.12g; Protein 45.61g

Ginger Beer Braised Pork Belly

Prep Time: 15 minutes | Cook Time: 50 minutes | Serves: 6

1 tablespoon vegetable, corn, or canola oil

900 g skinless pork belly, cut into 6 pieces

One 300 ml bottle non-alcoholic ginger beer

80 ml soy sauce, preferably reduced-sodium

80 ml fresh orange juice

4 medium spring onions, trimmed and cut into 2.5 cm pieces

2 tablespoons finely minced orange zest

1 medium garlic clove, peeled and minced (1 teaspoon)

2 tablespoons minced peeled fresh ginger

½ teaspoon ground cinnamon

2 star anise pods

1. Move slider to AIR FRY/STOVETOP. Select SEAR/SAUTÉ and set to Hi5. Select START/STOP to begin preheating. Allow unit to preheat for 1 minute. 2. After 1 minute, warm the oil in the pot for a minute or two. Add half the pork belly pieces and brown well on all sides, turning occasionally, about 10 minutes. Transfer these to a nearby bowl and brown the remaining pieces the same way before transferring them into that bowl. 3. Pour the ginger beer into the cooker and scrape up any browned bits on the pot's bottom. Press START/STOP to turn off the SEAR/SAUTÉ function. Then stir in the soy sauce, orange zest, orange juice, spring onions, ginger, cinnamon, garlic, and star anise pods. Return the pork belly pieces and any juices to the cooker. 4. Close the lid and move slider to PRESSURE. Make sure the pressure release valve is in the SEAL position. The temperature will default to HIGH, which is the correct setting. Set time to 35 minutes. Select START/STOP to begin cooking. 5. When cooking is complete, turn the pressure relief valve to the VENT position for quick pressure relief. Move slider to the right to unlock the lid, then carefully open it. 6. Transfer the pork belly to a serving platter or serving bowls. Find and discard the star anise pods. Use a flatware tablespoon to skim the excess surface fat from the sauce. Chunk up the meat, then spoon the sauce and spring onions over it in bowls.

Per Serving: Calories 884; Fat 85.07g; Sodium 265mg; Carbs 9.28g; Fibre 0.8g; Sugar 4.55g; Protein 15.83g

Savoury Beef Stew with Vegetables

Prep Time: 15 minutes | Cook Time: 35 minutes | Serves: 6

900 g beef stew meat (4 cm chunks)
1 tsp sea salt
½ tsp ground black pepper
½ tsp onion powder
40 g flour
3 tsp Italian seasoning, divided
2 tbsp olive oil
1 medium onion, quartered
4 cloves garlic, minced
2 tbsp balsamic vinegar or red wine
6 tbsp tomato paste

4 medium potatoes, peeled and chopped (2.5 cm chunks)
1 large sweet potato, peeled and chopped (2.5 cm chunks)
2 ribs celery, chopped
3 medium carrots, cut into slices
2 tsp Worcestershire sauce
1.2 L beef stock
1 bay leaf
2 tbsp fresh parsley, chopped (for garnish)

1. In a big bowl, mix together the salt, onion powder, pepper, flour and 1 teaspoon Italian seasoning. 2. Add the meat to the bowl, stir and rub all chunks with the spice mix. 3. Move slider to AIR FRY/STOVETOP. Select SEAR/SAUTÉ and set to 3. Select START/STOP to begin preheating. Allow unit to preheat for 2 minutes. After 2 minutes, add the oil and heat it up. 4. Add the meet and brown on all sides. 5. Remove the beef from the pot and place on a plate. 6. Add the onion and garlic to the pot and sauté for 1-2 minutes. 7. Pour in the balsamic vinegar and tomato paste and deglaze the pot by scraping the bottom to remove all of the brown bits. Press START/STOP to turn off the SEAR/SAUTÉ function. 8. Return the meat to the pot. Add the potatoes, celery, carrots, sweet potato, Worcestershire sauce, 2 teaspoons Italian seasoning, beef stock and bay leaf. Stir well. 9. Close the lid and move slider to PRESSURE. Make sure the pressure release valve is in the SEAL position. The temperature will default to HIGH, which is the correct setting. Set time to 25 minutes. Select START/STOP to begin cooking. 10. When cooking is complete, naturally release the pressure for 10 minutes. Then turn the pressure relief valve to the VENT position for quick pressure relief. Move slider to AIR FRY/ STOVETOP to unlock the lid, then carefully open it. 11. Top with fresh parsley and serve.

Per Serving: Calories 605; Fat 19.31g; Sodium 1211mg; Carbs 67.32g; Fibre 9.7g; Sugar 9.77g; Protein 43.24g

Pork Chops with Creamy Mushroom Gravy

Prep Time: 15 minutes | Cook Time: 40 minutes | Serves: 4

4 boneless pork loin chops
1 tsp onion powder
1 tsp salt
1 tsp black pepper
1 tsp garlic powder
1 tbsp paprika
¼ tsp cayenne pepper

2 tbsp coconut oil
½ medium onion, sliced
150 g baby bella mushrooms, sliced
1 tbsp butter
120 g heavy whipping cream
¼ – ½ tsp cornflour
1 tbsp chopped fresh parsley

1. Rinse the pork chops and pat dry with paper towel. 2. In a bowl, mix together the onion powder, black pepper, garlic powder, salt, paprika, and cayenne powder. 3. Season the pork chops with 1 tablespoon of the spice mix and rub all sides of the pork chops with the spice mix. 4. Move slider to AIR FRY/STOVETOP. Select SEAR/SAUTÉ and set to 3. Select START/STOP to begin preheating. Allow unit to preheat for 2 minutes. After 2 minutes, add and heat the oil. 5. Put the pork in the pot and cook for about 3 minutes on each side, until browned. 6. Transfer the meat to a plate and press START/STOP to turn off the SEAR/SAUTÉ function. 7. Add the onions and mushrooms to the pot. Place the pork chops on the top. 8. Close the lid and move slider to PRESSURE. Make sure the pressure release valve is in the SEAL position. The temperature will default to HIGH, which is the correct setting. Set time to 25 minutes. Select START/STOP to begin cooking. 9. When cooking is complete, naturally release the pressure for 10 minutes. Then turn the pressure relief valve to the VENT position for quick pressure relief. Move slider to AIR FRY/ STOVETOP to unlock the lid, then carefully open it. 10. Transfer the pork to a serving plate. 11. Move slider to AIR FRY/STOVETOP. Select SEAR/SAUTÉ and set to 3. Select START/STOP to begin cooking. add the heavy cream, butter, and remaining spice mix to the pot. Stir well. 12. Add the cornflour and mix well. Let the sauce simmer for 5 minutes until start to thicken. Press START/STOP. 13. Pour the gravy over the pork chops. Season with parsley and serve.

Per Serving: Calories 510; Fat 22.26g; Sodium 709mg; Carbs 35.29g; Fibre 5.9g; Sugar 1.67g; Protein 46.43g

Garlic Pork and Cabbage Stew

Prep Time: 10 minutes | Cook Time: 50 minutes | Serves: 8

1.8 kg. pork roast, cut into chunks
3 tbsp coconut oil
4 cloves garlic, minced
2 large onions, chopped

1 tsp salt
1 tsp ground black pepper
240 ml water
1 head cabbage, chopped

1. Move slider to AIR FRY/STOVETOP. Select SEAR/SAUTÉ and set to 3. Select START/STOP to begin preheating. Allow unit to preheat for 2 minutes. After 2 minutes, add and heat the oil. 2. Add the garlic and onions and sauté for 5-6 minutes until the onion is translucent. 3. Put the pork chunks in the pot and cook for 5 minutes on all sides. 4. Season with salt and pepper and pour the water, stir well. 5. Press START/STOP to turn off the SEAR/SAUTÉ function. 6. Close the lid and move slider to PRESSURE. Make sure the pressure release valve is in the SEAL position. The temperature will default to HIGH, which is the correct setting. Set time to 35 minutes. Select START/STOP to begin cooking. 7. When cooking is complete, turn the pressure relief valve to the VENT position for quick pressure relief. Move slider to the right to unlock the lid, then carefully open it. 8. Cook on SEAR/SAUTÉ function and set the heat to 3. Add the cabbage, stir and bring to a simmer. 9. Simmer the dish for 5 minutes. Serve.

Per Serving: Calories 520; Fat 25.27g; Sodium 417mg; Carbs 9.45g; Fibre 2.2g; Sugar 4.32g; Protein 61.55g

Lamb and Vegetables Casserole

Prep Time: 15 minutes | Cook Time: 45 minutes | Serves: 4

455 g lamb stew meat, cubed
1 tbsp olive oil
3 cloves garlic, minced
2 tomatoes, chopped
455 g baby potatoes
2 carrots, chopped
1 onion, chopped
1 celery stalk, chopped

2 tbsp ketchup
2 tbsp red wine
480 ml chicken stock
1 tsp sweet paprika
1 tsp cumin, ground
¼ tsp oregano, dried
¼ tsp rosemary, dried
Salt and ground black pepper to taste

1. Move slider to AIR FRY/STOVETOP. Select SEAR/SAUTÉ and set to 3. Select START/STOP to begin preheating. Allow unit to preheat for 2 minutes. After 2 minutes, heat the oil. 2. Add the lamb and cook until the meat has turned light brown. 3. Add the garlic and sauté for 1 minute more. 4. Add all of the remaining ingredients and spices. Press START/STOP to turn off the SEAR/SAUTÉ function. 5. Close the lid and move slider to PRESSURE. Make sure the pressure release valve is in the SEAL position. The temperature will default to HIGH, which is the correct setting. Set time to 35 minutes. Select START/STOP to begin cooking. 6. When cooking is complete, naturally release the pressure for 10 minutes. Then turn the pressure relief valve to the VENT position for quick pressure relief. Move slider to AIR FRY/ STOVETOP to unlock the lid, then carefully open it. Serve.

Per Serving: Calories 368; Fat 11.37g; Sodium 361mg; Carbs 36.88g; Fibre 5.2g; Sugar 9.62g; Protein 30.07g

Spiced Pork and White Beans

Prep Time: 15 minutes | Cook Time: 62 minutes | Serves: 8

❖❖❖❖❖❖

1½ tbsp vegetable oil
1.3 kg. pork shoulder, cut into 4 cm pieces
1 large yellow onion, sliced
380 g dried white beans
1.4 L water or chicken stock
225 g tomatoes, chopped
2 tsp chili powder

Spices:

2½ tbsp paprika
1 tbsp onion powder
1 tbsp dried thyme
1 tbsp dried leaf oregano

2 tsp garlic, minced
105 g light brown sugar
1 sprig fresh thyme
2 tbsp Creole mustard
½ tsp ground black pepper
1 bay leaf
1 tsp salt

1 tbsp black pepper
1 tbsp cayenne pepper
2 tbsp garlic powder
2 tsp salt

❖❖❖❖❖❖

1. Combine all the spices in a small bowl. 2. Rub the pork pieces with spice mix until well coated. 3. Move slider to AIR FRY/STOVETOP. Select SEAR/SAUTÉ and set to 3. Select START/STOP to begin preheating. Allow unit to preheat for 2 minutes. After 2 minutes, add and heat the oil. 4. Add the pork and cook, stirring occasionally, for 4-5 minutes until the meat has turned light brown. You may have to do it in two batches. 5. Transfer the meat to a bowl. 6. Add the onion to the pot and sauté for 2 minutes. 7. Add the beans and pour in the water/stock, mix well. Deglaze the pot by scraping the bottom to remove all of the brown bits. Press START/STOP to turn off the SEAR/SAUTÉ function. 8. Close the lid and move slider to PRESSURE. Make sure the pressure release valve is in the SEAL position. The temperature will default to HIGH, which is the correct setting. Set time to 20 minutes. Select START/STOP to begin cooking. 9. When cooking is complete, naturally release the pressure for 15 minutes. Then turn the pressure relief valve to the VENT position for quick pressure relief. Move slider to AIR FRY/ STOVETOP to unlock the lid, then carefully open it. 10. Add the tomatoes, garlic, chili powder, light brown sugar, mustard, black pepper, thyme, bay leaf and return pork to the pot. Stir. 11. Close the lid and cook at HIGH pressure for 20 minutes. 12. When the timer beeps, use a natural release for 15 minutes. Open the lid. 13. Cook on SEAR/SAUTÉ function and set the heat to 3, bring to a simmer and season with salt. Simmer for 10 minutes. Serve.

Per Serving: Calories 723; Fat 35.27g; Sodium 1634mg; Carbs 40.96g; Fibre 10.5g; Sugar 3.69g; Protein 60.09g

Red Velvet Cake Bites with Cream Cheese Frosting

Prep Time: 15 minutes | Cook Time: 12 minutes | Serves: 4

Nonstick cooking spray
240 ml water
180 g plain flour
35 g unsweetened cocoa powder
1 teaspoon baking powder
1 teaspoon baking soda
¼ teaspoon salt
150 g granulated sugar
120 ml buttermilk

4 tablespoons plus 2 tablespoons unsalted butter, at room temperature, divided
1 large egg
2 tablespoons plain unsweetened Greek yogurt
1 teaspoon red food colouring
115 g icing sugar
100 g cream cheese, at room temperature
1 tablespoon heavy cream
¼ teaspoon vanilla extract

1. Spray the cups of two silicone egg molds with nonstick cooking spray. 2. Pour the water into the pot and place the Deluxe Reversible Rack in the lower position in the pot. 3. In a medium bowl, whisk together the flour, baking powder, baking soda, cocoa powder, and salt. 4. In a big bowl, whisk together the egg, granulated sugar, buttermilk, 4 tablespoons of butter, and yogurt with a hand mixer until smooth. 5. Add the dry ingredients to the wet ingredients and mix with the hand mixer until well combined. Add the red food colouring and beat until the colour is fully incorporated into the batter. 6. Fill the cups of the egg molds halfway with batter. Lay a paper towel over the top of each mold (this will help catch excess moisture from the steam inside the pot), then cover the paper towel and egg bite molds loosely with aluminum foil. 7. Stack the two molds on top of each other and place on the rack inside the pot. 8. Close the lid and move slider to PRESSURE. Make sure the pressure release valve is in the SEAL position. The temperature will default to HIGH, which is the correct setting. Set time to 12 minutes. Select START/STOP to begin cooking. 9. When cooking is complete, naturally release the pressure for 30 minutes. Then turn the pressure relief valve to the VENT position for quick pressure relief. Move slider to AIR FRY/ STOVETOP to unlock the lid, then carefully open it. 10. Remove the molds from the pot and cool on a wire rack before using a spoon or butter knife to remove the cake bites from the molds. 11. While the cake bites are cooling, in a small bowl, whip the icing sugar, heavy cream, cream cheese, remaining 2 tablespoons of butter, and vanilla together with the hand mixer until fluffy, about 1 minute. 12. Dip each cake bite halfway into the cream cheese frosting.
Per Serving: Calories 556; Fat 20.31g; Sodium 659mg; Carbs 87.27g; Fibre 3.4g; Sugar 46.02g; Protein 10.63g

Cinnamon Fruit Compote

Prep Time: 15 minutes | Cook Time: 11 minutes | Serves: 6

240 ml apple juice
240 ml dry white wine
2 tablespoons honey
1 cinnamon stick
¼ teaspoon ground nutmeg

1 tablespoon grated lemon zest
1½ tablespoons grated orange zest
3 large apples, peeled, cored, and chopped
3 large pears, peeled, cored, and chopped
60 g dried cherries

1. Place all ingredients in the pot and stir well. Close the lid and move slider to PRESSURE. Make sure the pressure release valve is in the SEAL position. The temperature will default to HIGH, which is the correct setting. Set time to 1 minute. Select START/STOP to begin cooking. 2. When cooking is complete, turn the pressure relief valve to the VENT position for quick pressure relief. Move slider to the right to unlock the lid, then carefully open it. 3. Use a slotted spoon to transfer fruit to a serving bowl. Remove and discard cinnamon stick. Move slider to AIR FRY/STOVETOP. Select SEAR/SAUTÉ and set to Hi5. Select START/STOP to begin cooking. Bring juice in the pot to a boil. Cook, stirring constantly, until reduced to a syrup that will coat the back of a spoon, about 10 minutes. 4. Stir syrup into fruit mixture. Allow to cool slightly, then cover with plastic wrap and refrigerate overnight.

Per Serving: Calories 228; Fat 4.41g; Sodium 298mg; Carbs 46.52g; Fibre 6.8g; Sugar 34.56g; Protein 4.94g

Classic Applesauce

Prep Time: 15 minutes | Cook Time: 4 minutes | Serves: 16

1.3 kg apples, cored, cut into large chunks
80 ml water

1 tablespoon freshly squeezed lemon juice

1. Combine the apples, water, and lemon juice in the pot. Close the lid and move slider to PRESSURE. Make sure the pressure release valve is in the SEAL position. The temperature will default to HIGH, which is the correct setting. Set time to 4 minutes. Select START/STOP to begin cooking. 2. When cooking is complete, naturally release the pressure for 10 minutes. Then turn the pressure relief valve to the VENT position for quick pressure relief. Move slider to AIR FRY/ STOVETOP to unlock the lid, then carefully open it. 3. Using a potato masher, mash the apples to your desired chunkiness. Using a pair of tongs or a fork, transfer the apple peels to a deep, narrow container and blend using an immersion blender. Return to the pot and stir to combine. 4. Store in the fridge for up to 4 weeks in a covered container.

Per Serving: Calories 44; Fat 0.15g; Sodium 1mg; Carbs 11.81g; Fibre 2g; Sugar 8.86g; Protein 0.22g

Cinnamon Plums with Greek Yogurt

Prep Time: 15 minutes | Cook Time: 3 minutes | Serves: 6

❖ ❖ ❖ ❖ ❖ ❖

240 g dried plums
480 ml water
2 tablespoons sugar

2 cinnamon sticks
720 g low-fat plain Greek yogurt

❖ ❖ ❖ ❖ ❖ ❖

1. Add the dried plums, sugar, water, and cinnamon to the pot. 2. Close the lid and move slider to PRESSURE. Make sure the pressure release valve is in the SEAL position. The temperature will default to HIGH, which is the correct setting. Set time to 3 minutes. Select START/STOP to begin cooking. 3. When the timer beeps, turn the pressure relief valve to the VENT position for quick pressure relief. Move slider to the right to unlock the lid, then carefully open it. 4. Remove and discard cinnamon sticks. Serve warm over Greek yogurt.

Per Serving: Calories 204; Fat 2.04g; Sodium 112mg; Carbs 41.96g; Fibre 1.6g; Sugar 40.03g; Protein 6.93g

Oats Lemon Bars

Prep Time: 15 minutes | Cook Time: 12 minutes | Serves: 6

❖ ❖ ❖ ❖ ❖ ❖

60 g gluten-free rolled oats
75 g almond flour
60 ml melted coconut oil
2 tablespoons honey, plus 50 g
1 teaspoon vanilla extract

¼ teaspoon salt , divided
2 large eggs, beaten
Zest and juice of 2 lemons
1 teaspoon cornflour

❖ ❖ ❖ ❖ ❖ ❖

1. Line a square cake pan that fits the pot with aluminum foil. 2. In a medium bowl, mix together the oats, almond flour, coconut oil, the vanilla, 2 tablespoons of honey, and ⅛ teaspoon of salt to form a stiff dough. Press the dough into the bottom of the prepared pan. 3. In a separate bowl, whisk together the eggs, lemon zest and juice, honey, cornflour, and the remaining ⅛ teaspoon of salt. Pour the mixture over the crust. Cover the pan with foil. 4. Pour 240 ml of water into the pot and place the bottom layer of the Deluxe Reversible Rack in the lower position in the pot. Place the pan on top of the rack and close the lid. 5. Move slider to PRESSURE. Make sure the pressure release valve is in the SEAL position. The temperature will default to HIGH, which is the correct setting. Set time to 12 minutes. Select START/STOP to begin cooking. 6. When the cook time is complete, let the pressure release naturally for 15 minutes, then quick release any remaining pressure. 7. Carefully open the lid and lift out the pan. Chill the lemon bars in the refrigerator for at least 2 hours before slicing them into six portions and serving.

Per Serving: Calories 477; Fat 11.53g; Sodium 105mg; Carbs 102.73g; Fibre 2.1g; Sugar 93.5g; Protein 3.36g

Vanilla Pear Butter

Prep Time: 10 minutes | Cook Time: 35 minutes | Serves: 6

6 medium Bartlett pears, peeled, cored, and diced
60 ml dry white wine
1 tablespoon lemon juice
60 g sugar
2 orange slices
1 lemon slice

2 whole cloves
1 vanilla bean, split lengthwise
1 cinnamon stick
¼ teaspoon ground cardamom
⅛ teaspoon salt

1. Add pears, lemon juice and wine to the pot. Close the lid and move slider to PRESSURE. Make sure the pressure release valve is in the SEAL position. The temperature will default to HIGH, which is the correct setting. Set time to 8 minutes. Select START/STOP to begin cooking. 2. When cooking is complete, naturally release the pressure for 10 minutes. Then turn the pressure relief valve to the VENT position for quick pressure relief. Move slider to AIR FRY/ STOVETOP to unlock the lid, then carefully open it. 3. Transfer fruit and juices to a blender or food processor, and purée until smooth. 4. Return purée to the pot and add sugar. Move slider to AIR FRY/STOVETOP. Select SEAR/SAUTÉ and set to 3. Select START/STOP to begin cooking. Cook until sugar dissolves, about 1 minute. Stir in orange slices, vanilla bean, cinnamon stick, cloves, cardamom, and salt. Cook until mixture thickens and mounds slightly on spoon, about 25 minutes. 5. Remove and discard orange and lemon slices, cloves, and cinnamon stick. Remove vanilla pod and slice in half. Use the back of a knife to scrape away any vanilla seeds still clinging to the pod and stir them into the pear butter. 6. Cool and refrigerate covered for up to 10 days or freeze for up to 4 months.
Per Serving: Calories 154; Fat 1.41g; Sodium 129mg; Carbs 34.33g; Fibre 6.2g; Sugar 22.85g; Protein 1.85g

Tasty Peanut Butter Pudding

Prep Time: 15 minutes | Cook Time: 18 minutes | Serves: 4

480 ml
60 g sugar
2 tablespoons cornflour
¼ teaspoon salt

100 g creamy peanut butter
1 teaspoon vanilla extract
240 ml water

1. Move slider to AIR FRY/STOVETOP. Select SEAR/SAUTÉ and set to 3. Select START/STOP to begin preheating. Allow unit to preheat for 2 minutes. After 2 minutes, whisk the milk, cornflour, sugar, and salt together in the pot. Simmer, whisking frequently until it starts to bubble, about 7 minutes. 2. Whisk in the peanut butter and vanilla until the peanut butter is melted and mixed in completely. Press START/STOP to turn off the SEAR/SAUTÉ function. Transfer the pudding to a heat-safe bowl (I use a glass bowl) and cover with aluminum foil. 3. When the pot is cool enough to handle, wash and dry it. Pour the water into the pot and place the Deluxe Reversible Rack in the lower position in the pot. Place the bowl of pudding on the rack. 4. Close the lid and move slider to PRESSURE. Make sure the pressure release valve is in the SEAL position. The temperature will default to HIGH, which is the correct setting. Set time to 8 minutes. Select START/STOP to begin cooking. 5. When cooking is complete, turn the pressure relief valve to the VENT position for quick pressure relief. Move slider to the right to unlock the lid, then carefully open it. 6. Carefully remove the bowl from the pot and stir the pudding. Let it cool on the counter, then serve.
Per Serving: Calories 316; Fat 20.14g; Sodium 345mg; Carbs 25.59g; Fibre 2g; Sugar 15.18g; Protein 11.27g

Vanilla Almond Milk

Prep Time: 10 minutes | Cook Time: 1 minute | Serves: 6

❖❖❖❖❖❖

120 g raw almonds
1.1 L filtered water, divided

1 teaspoon vanilla bean paste
½ teaspoon pumpkin pie spice

❖❖❖❖❖❖

1. Add almonds and 240 ml water to the pot. Close the lid and move slider to PRESSURE. Make sure the pressure release valve is in the SEAL position. The temperature will default to HIGH, which is the correct setting. Set time to 1 minute. Select START/STOP to begin cooking. 2. When the timer beeps, turn the pressure relief valve to the VENT position for quick pressure relief. Move slider to the right to unlock the lid, then carefully open it. Strain almonds and rinse under cool water. Transfer to a high-powered blender with remaining water. Purée for 2 minutes on high speed. 3. Pour mixture into a nut milk bag set over a big bowl. Squeeze bag to extract all liquid. Stir in vanilla and pumpkin pie spice. 4. Transfer to a Mason jar or sealed jug and refrigerate for 8 hours. Stir or shake gently before serving.

Per Serving: Calories 4; Fat 0.12g; Sodium 5mg; Carbs 0.71g; Fibre 0.1g; Sugar 0.4g; Protein 0.12g

Lemony Cinnamon Apples

Prep Time: 10 minutes | Cook Time: 4 minutes | Serves: 4

❖❖❖❖❖❖

1 tablespoon coconut oil
5 medium apples, peeled, cored, and cut into large chunks

1½ teaspoons ground cinnamon
1 tablespoon water
1 tablespoon lemon juice

❖❖❖❖❖❖

1. Move slider to AIR FRY/STOVETOP. Select SEAR/SAUTÉ and set to 3. Select START/STOP to begin preheating. Allow unit to preheat for 2 minutes. 2. After 2 minutes, heat the oil for 1 minute, add the apples, water, cinnamon, and lemon juice and stir to combine. Press START/STOP to turn off the SEAR/SAUTÉ function. 3. Close the lid and move slider to PRESSURE. Make sure the pressure release valve is in the SEAL position. The temperature will default to HIGH, which is the correct setting. Set time to 1 minute. Select START/STOP to begin cooking. 4. When cooking is complete, turn the pressure relief valve to the VENT position for quick pressure relief. Move slider to the right to unlock the lid, then carefully open it. Serve warm.

Per Serving: Calories 151; Fat 3.81g; Sodium 2mg; Carbs 32.47g; Fibre 6g; Sugar 23.75g; Protein 0.64g

Blueberry Oats Crisp

Prep Time: 15 minutes | Cook Time: 17 minutes | Serves: 4

For the Filling:

1 (250 g) bag frozen blueberries
2 tablespoons fresh orange juice
15 g erythritol

1 teaspoon pure vanilla extract
2 tablespoons almond flour
1 teaspoon orange zest

For the Topping:

100 g almond flour
15 g erythritol
80 g old fashioned rolled oats
60 g sliced almonds

1½ teaspoons pure vanilla extract
60 ml coconut oil
2 tablespoons fresh orange juice

1. To make the Filling: In a medium bowl, mix together the filling ingredients and transfer to a cake pan that fits the pot, set aside. 2. To make the Topping: In another bowl, mix together the topping ingredients. Use your hands to incorporate the oil into the rest of the ingredients evenly. 3. Pour the topping over the blueberry filling. 4. Pour 480 ml water into the pot and place the Deluxe Reversible Rack in the lower position in the pot. Place the cake pan on the rack. 5. Close the lid and move slider to PRESSURE. Make sure the pressure release valve is in the SEAL position. The temperature will default to HIGH, which is the correct setting. Set time to 17 minutes. Select START/ STOP to begin cooking. 6. When cooking is complete, turn the pressure relief valve to the VENT position for quick pressure relief. Move slider to the right to unlock the lid, then carefully open it. 7. Spoon into four bowls and serve.
Per Serving: Calories 976; Fat 24.9g; Sodium 16mg; Carbs 205.04g; Fibre 42.1g; Sugar 136.08g; Protein 10.36g

Simple Strawberry Compote

Prep Time: 15 minutes | Cook Time: 4 minutes | Serves: 6

700 g frozen strawberries
50 g sugar

1 tablespoon freshly squeezed lemon juice

1. Combine the strawberries, sugar, and lemon juice in the pot. Stir to coat the berries. Close the lid and move slider to PRESSURE. Make sure the pressure release valve is in the SEAL position. The temperature will default to HIGH, which is the correct setting. Set time to 4 minutes. Select START/STOP to begin cooking. 2. When cooking is complete, naturally release the pressure for 10 minutes. Then turn the pressure relief valve to the VENT position for quick pressure relief. Move slider to AIR FRY/ STOVETOP to unlock the lid, then carefully open it. 3. Using a potato masher, mash the berries until they are broken down completely. Pour into a container and chill. The compote will thicken as it cools. 4. Store in the fridge for up to 4 weeks in a covered container.
Per Serving: Calories 68; Fat 0.17g; Sodium 3mg; Carbs 17.78g; Fibre 3.1g; Sugar 10.86g; Protein 0.64g

Easy Cinnamon Pineapple

Prep Time: 10 minutes | Cook Time: 5 minutes | Serves: 6

✦✦✦✦✦✦

2 tablespoons coconut oil

1 large pineapple, cored and cut into 6 cm pieces

1½ teaspoons ground cinnamon

✦✦✦✦✦✦

1. Move slider to AIR FRY/STOVETOP. Select SEAR/SAUTÉ and set to 3. Select START/STOP to begin preheating. Allow unit to preheat for 2 minutes. 2. After 2 minutes, heat the oil for 1 minute, add the pineapple and cinnamon and stir to combine. Press START/STOP to turn off the SEAR/SAUTÉ function. 3. Close the lid and move slider to PRESSURE. Make sure the pressure release valve is in the SEAL position. The temperature will default to HIGH, which is the correct setting. Set time to 2 minutes. Select START/STOP to begin cooking. 4. When cooking is complete, turn the pressure relief valve to the VENT position for quick pressure relief. Move slider to the right to unlock the lid, then carefully open it.

Per Serving: Calories 116; Fat 4.76g; Sodium 2mg; Carbs 20.26g; Fibre 2.7g; Sugar 13.86g; Protein 0.94g

Homemade Walnut Brownies

Prep Time: 15 minutes | Cook Time: 50 minutes | Serves: 6

✦✦✦✦✦✦

Nonstick cooking spray

360 ml water

200 g sugar

65 g plain flour

35 g unsweetened cocoa powder

¼ teaspoon baking powder

8 tablespoons unsalted butter, melted

2 large eggs

½ teaspoon vanilla extract

60 g chopped walnuts

✦✦✦✦✦✦

1. Spray a heat-safe bowl that fits the pot with nonstick cooking spray. 2. Pour the water into the pot and place the Deluxe Reversible Rack in the lower position in the pot. 3. In a medium bowl, mix together the flour, cocoa powder, sugar, and baking powder. 4. In a large bowl, whisk together the eggs, melted butter, and vanilla. 5. Add the dry ingredients to the wet ingredients and mix until well combined. Fold in the chopped walnuts. 6. Pour the batter into the prepared heat-safe bowl and smooth the top with a spatula. Lay a paper towel over the top of the bowl (this will help catch excess moisture from the steam inside the pot), then cover the paper towel and bowl loosely with aluminum foil. Place the bowl on the rack the pot. 7. Close the lid and move slider to PRESSURE. Make sure the pressure release valve is in the SEAL position. The temperature will default to HIGH, which is the correct setting. Set time to 50 minutes. Select START/STOP to begin cooking. 8. When cooking is complete, naturally release the pressure for 10 minutes. Then turn the pressure relief valve to the VENT position for quick pressure relief. Move slider to AIR FRY/ STOVETOP to unlock the lid, then carefully open it. 9. Carefully remove the bowl from the pot and cool on a wire rack before slicing.

Per Serving: Calories 270; Fat 16.9g; Sodium 12mg; Carbs 28.61g; Fibre 2.1g; Sugar 16.66g; Protein 4.46g

Vanilla Wine Poached Apricots

Prep Time: 5 minutes | Cook Time: 1 minute | Serves: 6

❖❖❖❖❖❖

300 ml water
60 g marsala wine
50 g sugar

1 teaspoon vanilla bean paste
8 medium apricots, sliced in half and pitted

❖❖❖❖❖❖

1. Place all ingredients in the pot. Stir to combine. Close the lid and move slider to PRESSURE. Make sure the pressure release valve is in the SEAL position. The temperature will default to HIGH, which is the correct setting. Set time to 1 minute. Select START/STOP to begin cooking. 2. When cooking is complete, turn the pressure relief valve to the VENT position for quick pressure relief. Move slider to the right to unlock the lid, then carefully open it. 3. Let stand for 10 minutes. Carefully remove apricots from poaching liquid with a slotted spoon. Serve warm or at room temperature.

Per Serving: Calories 31; Fat 0.03g; Sodium 4mg; Carbs 7.75g; Fibre 0.4g; Sugar 7.05g; Protein 0.28g

Conclusion

Most people are familiar with the Ninja Kitchen System, but the Ninja Foodi MAX Multi-Cooker is a bit different. The Multi-Cooker is a countertop appliance that can slow cook, steam, and sear/sauté. The Ninja MAX Multi-Cooker is a great addition to any kitchen, and it's especially handy if you have limited counter space. It's easy to use, and the built-in strainer is a major time saver. If you're looking for a versatile appliance that can do it all, the Ninja MAX Multi-Cooker is a perfect choice.

Printed in Great Britain
by Amazon